# Unlock Your PhD Potential

*Unlock Your PhD Potential* is a comprehensive guide designed to help you overcome the hurdles of securing and succeeding in a PhD programme. The book demystifies the doctoral journey, offering step-by-step advice on navigating applications, funding, and the challenges of academic life, while prioritising equity, diversity, inclusion, and mental well-being. Written by an expert in psychology, it empowers readers to approach their doctorate with confidence and resilience, highlighting how successfully navigating human relationships is central to PhD success.

Packed with actionable insights, the guide covers everything from choosing the right supervisor and managing work-life balance to combating procrastination and imposter syndrome. Drawing on decades of experience mentoring students from diverse backgrounds, as well as on her research expertise in the psychology of discrimination and structural barriers, Prof. Zagefka combines academic expertise with practical, real-world advice. Whether you are preparing to apply or already deep into your doctoral studies, this book offers essential strategies for excelling at every stage.

*Unlock Your PhD Potential* is ideal for prospective and current PhD students in the UK and beyond, including international applicants and those from traditionally underrepresented backgrounds. Academic advisors and supervisors will also find it an invaluable resource for supporting doctoral researchers. With its accessible language and expert insight, it is your roadmap to academic success.

**Hanna Zagefka** is Dean of the Faculty of Science at Royal Holloway, University of London, and former Head of its outstanding Department of Psychology with its vibrant PhD community. With over 20 years of experience supervising students from a wide range of backgrounds – including first-generation, women, ethnic minority, LGBTQ+, and international students from Africa, Asia, and the Americas – she brings rare, first-hand insight into PhD life. A social psychologist specialising in identity, discrimination, and human relationships, Prof. Zagefka combines academic leadership, supervisory experience, and psychological expertise to offer practical, empowering advice that enables students to thrive in their PhD journey.

# Unlock Your PhD Potential

## A Practical and Inclusive Guide to Securing, Navigating, and Excelling in Your Doctoral Journey

**Hanna Zagefka**

LONDON AND NEW YORK

Designed cover image: Getty Images

First published 2026
by Routledge
4 Park Square, Milton Park, Abingdon, Oxon OX14 4RN

and by Routledge
605 Third Avenue, New York, NY 10158

*Routledge is an imprint of the Taylor & Francis Group, an informa business*



*British Library Cataloguing-in-Publication Data*
A catalogue record for this book is available from the British Library

ISBN: 978-1-041-03130-7 (hbk)
ISBN: 978-1-041-04812-1 (pbk)
ISBN: 978-1-003-63007-4 (ebk)

DOI: 10.4324/9781003630074

Typeset in Times New Roman
by SPi Technologies India Pvt Ltd (Straive)

# Contents

# Acknowledgements

The ideas in this book draw on my first-hand experience and on insights from social psychological research, particularly findings on how people think, decide, and behave – insights that apply directly to work design and to the realities of PhD life. I have also been influenced by popular science writing, especially Oliver Burkeman's work on making meaningful use of limited time. Several practices discussed here, including the idea of keeping a 'done list' alongside a 'to do' list, stem from his writing and have been personally transformative.

I have learned as much from my PhD students (and PGT students and PostDocs) as they have from me. Supervising doctoral researchers has deepened my understanding of different cultural and political contexts and sharpened my appreciation of the human dynamics involved in supportive, respectful collaboration. I am deeply grateful to my students for their trust, generosity, and the shared enjoyment of our intellectual journey, and it is a pleasure to see them thrive in their diverse careers. There are too many to credit every student who would deserve this, but particular shout-outs to Abdinasir, Chuma, Diana, Emine, Gehad, Leonie, Limabenla, Linda, Lucia, Nali, Sam K, Siugmin, and Trevor – you have broadened my horizon and changed my world.

I am indebted to my own PhD supervisor Rupert, whose commitment to thoughtful and supportive mentorship has shaped my own approach to supervision. I have learned so much from you. I was – and continue to be – lucky to have you in my life.

Declaration: AI (ChatGPT) was used to analyse the themes that emerged from the interviews I conducted with my students, described in Chapter 6.

# 1 Introduction

So, you are interested in doing a PhD? Excellent choice! Doing a PhD can be interesting and fun, and completing one is a prestigious achievement and good for your job prospects inside and outside of academia. You might be vaguely aware of this, but still a bit hazy on what exactly a PhD entails. So, to begin with, let's look at what a PhD actually is.

## What is a PhD?

'PhD' stands for Doctor of Philosophy. This is misleading though, because you can do a PhD in virtually any subject, not only philosophy! You can hold a PhD in physics, sociology, drama, psychology, and so on and a whole array of other subjects. It is a postgraduate degree and, therefore, more advanced than the undergraduate degrees such as a BA or BSc, and more advanced than lower-level Postgraduate Degrees like an MA or MSc. A PhD is the highest academic qualification that exists, and as such, it carries significant prestige.

There are some differences to the structure of a typical PhD programme in different countries, but irrespective of national context a PhD is universally accepted as the highest recognition of academic competence. The discussion here will mainly focus on the UK academic system when describing the PhD journey. A PhD in the UK typically involves students conducting original and significant research, advancing the boundaries of knowledge, resulting in a publication-worthy thesis. The work is conducted under the supervision of one academic line manager who acts as advisor and mentor, although an increasingly popular model is to have a supervisory team consisting of two or even more academics. There is usually a high degree of independence and autonomy in the way PhD students are expected to work – the supervisors provide guidance but do not normally dictate the direction of the work. The direction is meant to be set by the student, with the PhD thesis being an original contribution to knowledge by the student. As such, the role of the supervisor is to support, not to lead the intellectual endeavour.

DOI: 10.4324/9781003630074-1

A PhD in the UK typically takes 3–4 years. In the UK, the process can exceed four years typically only when the student is registered as part-time. Many people embark on a PhD after having studied for three years for an undergraduate BSc or BA, followed by another year studying towards a postgraduate degree such as an MSc or MA. Some people enter a PhD programme straight after completing their BSc/BA, and some people go into paid employment outside of university after their undergraduate degree, only to return years later to start their PhD. The written piece of work resulting from such a long time of intensive investigation is usually substantive, amounting to hundreds of pages. In the UK, most of the work will be independent research conducted by the student, although there might be (depending on the institution) some seminars and classroom teaching activities that are a compulsory part of the PhD training. This might, depending on the setup and funding model, entail both taking and delivering classroom teaching activities – some studentships are tied to an expectation that the PhD student contributes to undergraduate teaching, for example. The emphasis on receiving instruction via classroom teaching can be more pronounced in some countries such as the USA and less pronounced in some others such as the UK. Some PhD places are funded: the student obtains a scholarship either from the university or another agency such as a research council or government funding in the home country. This usually consists of a commitment to cover the student's tuition fees as well as a monthly stipend to cover living expenses. Other PhD places are self-funded, and the student works alongside their studies to support themselves. The issue of funding will be discussed in more detail in Chapter 2.

## What does the PhD work entail? A very brief overview

So, what would you typically be doing during your PhD? This of course depends on your chosen subject, but the end product will be an original, independent, and significant piece of research in a specific field of study. As mentioned elsewhere, the process of doing a PhD can differ slightly between countries, and what is described here focuses on the UK. This means you will identify a question that has not yet been answered – the work should address a gap in our knowledge base in order for the PhD to make a novel contribution. You will need to have some kind of rudimentary understanding of where this gap might be in order to even write your PhD proposal. However, once you get started, your first task will be to develop a much more nuanced understanding of the literature and its limitations – you are likely to dive quite deep into the existing science or literature to begin with.

In the natural and social sciences, you are then likely to move on to the empirical part of your degree: designing and running experiments, surveys, interviews, or focus groups. The emphasis will be on collecting new data and analysing that data, in order to address the question you've set out to answer. Some PhDs can be focused on the analysis of secondary (already existing) data, and some PhD theses might be theoretical in focus and not entail data collection – this is especially true in the humanities.

For those PhDs that are empirical in nature (i.e., that rely on the collection and analysis of data), for example in psychology, you are likely to conduct a series of studies, not only one. How many studies exactly are expected will depend on several factors: how time-consuming is the data collection? If you are working with difficult-to-reach populations and need to spend considerable time reaching your target samples, this will be taken into account. If you are collecting longitudinal data, which can be difficult and time-consuming, that will also be taken into account. If you are collecting data via online platforms, which allow the collection of data from large samples very quickly, this will also affect expectations. If your effect sizes are small and you subsequently need very large samples to investigate your chosen question, this will also be considered. It clearly takes more to conduct a study with 10,000 participants than to conduct a study with 20 participants! To give some sense of the scope of the work, a typical academic PhD in psychology might comprise around 3–10 studies (note that the expectations for vocationally focused PhDs, such as a DClinPsy, are different yet again). This means that, on average, you would be looking to design, conduct, analyse, and write up about 1–4 studies per year over the course of your PhD.

The traditional format of conducting a PhD was to leave the write-up until the end. Students would often focus solely on the empirical part and then reserve 6–8 months in the last year to writing up the work. Thankfully, the advent of a new PhD format, 'by publication,' has sparked improvements. A PhD 'by publication' results in a thesis where peer-reviewed journal articles make up the different chapters. This means that each chapter has its own literature list, introduction, and conclusion, and there might be some overlap between chapters. For example, the same paper might be foundational to several chapters, and be cited several times, or a key concept might be explained in several chapter introductions, whereas in the older format it might only have been covered once in the general introduction. The aspiration is that some of the chapters/peer-reviewed articles will be published before the end of the PhD, giving the student a vital boost to their CV if the goal is to find employment within academia. However, this is usually not a requirement; it is sufficient that the work is written up in a format that could potentially be submitted, and it is often not mandatory for the work to have been submitted or even accepted for publication.

There are several advantages to writing a PhD by publication, or in any case to writing up your work as you go along. As noted, this format makes it easier to turn your work into something that can be disseminated via outlets that reach a wider audience, such as peer-reviewed journals. In theory, PhD theses themselves are also publicly available documents, usually accessible to any interested reader via the home institution's library. In practice, it is rare for someone to go digging up a PhD thesis – if you want your work to be read and to have an impact, it is worth publishing it via other channels that reach more people. The format also helps with potential writers' block by dividing up the writing work into more bite-sized chunks and by staggering it. Writing a little bit, every now and then, is easier than being faced with a six-month period solely dedicated to producing 60,000 words or so! Last but not least, writing can help facilitate mental, logical, and analytical clarity. Writing up the work as you go along can assist in clarifying outstanding issues and where to take your work next to address those.

One decision PhD students need to make during the course of their work is about the trade-off between depth versus breadth. Some of my students have investigated essentially just one question, looking at it from different angles and with different methods. They have gained an understanding of their chosen phenomenon in minute detail. Other students have been more expansive in their interests and have at times pursued so many different lines of enquiry that it is a major job to find the common thread between them and to tie it all together in one overarching framework. At the end of the day, the product will need to be one coherent thesis with one title encompassing all the content. A focus on depth and on breadth can both work; you will need to work out which approach is best for you. In this context, it is also important to acknowledge that PhDs sometimes get re-focused: I know many a student who put their first couple of empirical studies in the bin, because after learning more about the literature and state of the science in their area, they decided to go down a different path of enquiry. This is totally fine – a PhD is about a learning process; it is not about linear progress towards a perfect end result.

Some PhD funding schemes now have an integral component of an industry placement that forms part of the PhD experience. The placement should be in an industry that is related to the theoretical PhD work – for example, a PhD on child development could involve a placement in a school, the Department for Education, social services, and so on. Placements enrich the PhD learning experience and equip the student with essential workplace experience, thereby enhancing employability skills and later employment prospects. Much is to be gained from leaving the ivory tower of higher education and getting exposure to different organisations, norms, and contexts.

Many PhD programmes also explicitly encourage students to engage in methods training. This might be training offered at the home institution, at a partner institution within the same doctoral training network, or training offered through UKRI (UK Research and Innovation, the national funding agency for research and innovation in the UK). Training might focus on research methods and skills such as qualitative or quantitative methods, lab-based approaches, or fieldwork, or on coding, data analysis, and inferential statistics. It might also be focused on professional and transferable skills (e.g., presentation or project management skills), training in impact and public engagement, entrepreneurship and innovation training, or training in issues related to equity, diversity, and inclusion (EDI). Many students are lucky to benefit from a diverse range of offers and are well advised to make the most of it.

Ideally, PhD study also entails participation in academic conferences where colleagues present their latest work (often in progress or not yet published). These can be brilliant opportunities to get a sense of the state of the art and latest debates within a field, to network with peers (many conferences specifically include early-career networking events in their programmes), and to get exposure and be noticed by some of the leading academics in the field (who might sit on academic hiring panels in the future). But, even for students who do not have ambitions towards an academic career and who plan to leave for industry after completion of the PhD, attending an academic conference can be an enriching and enjoyable experience. Most students will need some advice from their mentors in terms of which conference will be the most useful investment of time and funds. This will vary from field to field, but as a general rule, my impression is that students tend to get more out of smaller events with more opportunities for connecting with participants. Large conferences with thousands of participants tend to be more challenging to navigate for many students.

The ultimate step of the PhD journey, after the entire body of work has been written up and submitted, is the examination by experts in the field. The purpose of this is to check that the PhD makes a sufficiently novel contribution to the field and that it is the genuine work of the candidate (and not plagiarised or presenting someone else's ideas). This quality check is universal in higher education, but the exact form it takes differs between different countries. In the UK, the check consists of a viva – an oral exam – conducted by an external examiner (an academic expert from a different university) and an internal examiner (from the candidate's home institution). The viva typically takes around 2–3 hours, although it can be much shorter or longer. One of my peers had a viva that lasted over two days! Luckily, nowadays there are usually checks in place to ensure that the stress induced by the exam is manageable. Many universities will have an independent chair observe the viva, a person who is responsible for ensuring that the process is fair, that regular breaks are offered, and so on.

Not all countries follow this viva format. In some countries (e.g., Australia or India), the exam consists of a written report/scoring of the work by externals; it is a paper-based exercise without face-to-face interaction. In some countries (e.g., Germany), the PhD supervisor themselves assesses the work. This, to me, seems bizarre: how can the same person who heavily shaped the work be sufficiently neutral to objectively assess it? In some countries (e.g., Netherlands, Belgium), the oral viva defence which happens behind closed doors in the UK is a public event, with members of the academic community and even friends and family of the candidate watching the event.

In many countries, the PhD thesis does not receive a mark as such, but the decision on quality is a pass-fail decision. In the UK, there are four potential outcomes from a PhD viva: fail (in reality, this hardly ever happens), pass with major corrections (the work is not deemed sufficient in itself and substantial revisions are required, e.g., conducting more empirical work), pass with minor corrections (these are less substantive changes that might be required, of a scope where revisions can be carried out usually within a couple of days to a month or so), and pass without corrections (again, this hardly ever happens, because most substantive works will have some at least minor ways in which they might be improved). In my experience, if the student and supervisors have done their job diligently, the most common outcome of a PhD viva is minor corrections, and if you are reasonably confident in the quality of your work, it is a realistic expectation that you might exit the PhD viva with this decision. Irrespective of the format of the examination itself and the range of possible decisions/outcomes (which differ between countries), in the vast majority of cases a PhD project will end in the successful, happy graduation of the candidate.

## Why do a PhD?

There are at least three broad reasons why someone might want to do a PhD. The first reason is the pleasure that comes from pursuing knowledge and understanding. Have you ever been utterly fascinated by a certain topic or problem, and motivated to immerse yourself completely in trying to understand as much about it as possible? If yes, just imagine being given a lot of time to delve as deep as you want into the subject matter. Imagine having extremely high levels of autonomy in directing your pursuit. Imagine someone even agrees to give you money to enable you to do this. If this sounds good to you, then you have a good mindset for a potential PhD candidate. If you find the idea of having incredible freedom to explore and learn in order to better understand the world (or a specific part of it) appealing, then a PhD might just be for you. If you find the chance of developing your work in a multitude of different possible directions exciting rather than daunting, you will make a great PhD candidate.

The second reason for doing a PhD is that it is an essential entry ticket for anyone aspiring to a research or teaching career in a university in a permanent capacity. Without having a PhD, a career as an academic is not possible. Working as an academic has many advantages. The constant exposure to new, innovative ideas and new generations of students can keep you young and mentally agile. The high control over your schedule can help you achieve a reasonable work-life balance. For sure, there are many factors that speak against choosing an academic career. Pressures are ever increasing, and the pay is not particularly competitive compared to industry. But, whatever the pros and cons of working in academia, this option is only open to those who have successfully completed a PhD.

But not everyone who undertakes PhD study aspires to be an academic. Many people embark on a PhD with a clear aim of leaving academia for industry afterwards, and an advanced academic degree promises many benefits. A third reason for doing a PhD is therefore the competitive edge you will gain on the job market outside the 'ivory tower' compared to peers who can only point to an undergraduate or lesser postgraduate degree. It also means that you might be able to enter the job market at a higher level of seniority than you otherwise would have done, and it can mean that you advance at a faster rate in industry too. You will be able to call yourself 'Dr' or 'Doctor,' which carries significant prestige. It also carries some potential for confusion, because many people don't realise that there are doctors other than medical doctors. So, if you are on a flight and there is a medical emergency and the staff ask whether there is a doctor on board, and you are a doctor of history or social work, it might just be best to keep stum, rather than having to explain that you are that 'other type' of doctor! Having said this, one reason for completing a PhD is that it can afford career advantages in any future occupational field and independent of the chosen industry.

Some of the career advantages are due to the fact that a PhD marks you out to potential employers as someone who is capable of very advanced learning and who has well-developed technical and/or transferable skills. Transferable skills that you can point to post-PhD are advanced analytical skills, written communication skills, research skills, presentation skills, problem-solving skills, autonomy of thought, creativity, and – depending on your field of study – maybe advanced numerical skills too. These can be useful assets to cite in many job applications. In addition, you might be able to cite advanced time management skills and the ability to work in self-directed ways and under pressure. Without a doubt, you will have established a proven track record that testifies to above-average grit. Where PhD students have also gathered experience in front-of-class teaching or collaborating with other members of a lab, they might, in addition, be able to point to leadership and teamwork skills. In sum, there are many transferable skills that a PhD can give you advanced training in, which you can justly cite when entering the job market outside the ivory tower. I personally know many PhD students who left academia to join industry and who did so at a higher level of seniority than they otherwise would have done, going straight into leadership positions rather than having to work their way up. I also know students who successfully navigated career shifts and entered new industries and fields which might have remained closed to them without the PhD degree under their belt. A PhD can be as helpful for career advancement outside the ivory tower as it is inside it.

In sum, then, there are at least three reasons for doing a PhD: the pleasure that comes with the pursuit of knowledge, an essential entry ticket for anyone aspiring to a career in academia, and a career-boosting move for those interested in working in industry. To this already persuasive list of arguments, we can add a couple of further ones, if we ponder what some famous philosophers have to say about the pursuit of knowledge. As emphasised by the English philosopher Sir Francis Bacon: knowledge is power. Advanced study can increase your social capital, the esteem in which others hold you, your bargaining prowess, your outcomes in life. It might make your parents proud. Moreover, according to the Prussian philosopher Humboldt, the acquisition of knowledge through higher study encourages the cultivation of intellectual and personal virtues, which are values in their own right. According to this view, the pursuit of intellectual and personal development is a fundamental virtue for anyone seeking to lead a 'good life,' and a morally responsible society has a duty to ensure its citizens have ongoing opportunities for self-education and growth. No matter whether you want to do a PhD because you consider broadening your horizon as a value onto itself or whether you consider it a means to another end such as career advancement, embarking on this journey can be a smart choice.

## PhD work and contribution to society

Ideas about the purpose of PhD study and higher education more broadly have undergone significant change in the UK in recent times. The purpose of doctoral level study is not only to educate and to advance knowledge through world-class research, but such pursuits are also expected to drive economic growth and societal progress. In other words, they are expected to make a positive contribution to society and the economy. This shift away from being purely education and research focused towards an expectation of having broader positive impact has also informed recent funding strategy. It does, however, sometimes feel or seem at odds with the endeavour to pursue scientifically excellent basic or fundamental research, which explores new concepts, mechanisms, and phenomena freely without a view to immediate application. Many academics feel such fundamental research is essential to drive unexpected, transformative discoveries: many major innovations – like electricity, antibiotics, or the internet – originated from fundamental discoveries with no initial application in mind. However, most funders in the UK these days want to know how PhD work will have a direct positive societal impact. This is a brief that is easily catered to for some disciplines (e.g., social work) and harder for others (e.g., pure maths). Irrespective of discipline, it will be a useful exercise for you to reflect on the question: what is the motivation for your PhD? What are you hoping to achieve? Are you motivated by pure scientific discovery, or are you hoping that your PhD work will make the world a better place, in a small way? Your private answer to this question might not be the same answer you give on a funding application. PhD applicants in the UK will need to think about how to position themselves vis-à-vis those expectations. In reality, most academic work can be argued to bring positive societal benefits, but many students need some support in identifying those narratives and teasing out those stories in ways that might appeal to funders. Irrespective of whether you applaud or object to the recent trend to evaluate the value of academic work through a neoliberal frame, i.e., through the lens of market contributions and economic returns, this context is reality and cannot be ignored by anyone engaged in higher education, whether as a student or educator.

## Why should you read a book about how to do a PhD?

If pursuing a PhD sounds interesting and you think you might want to give this advanced-level study a try, why then would you want to read the rest of this book? It is a sad fact that many people who would easily have the potential to succeed at a PhD do not even try, because they feel intimidated and lack confidence, maybe because they belong to a group that has suffered structural historic discrimination. It is also a sad fact that despite the many rewards and advantages that come with PhD study, each year a significant number of students drop out of their programme and admit defeat without obtaining the degree of PhD, and sometimes without obtaining any degree at all. Some students take an exit award of MPhil, which is a degree lesser than that of PhD, but some students leave without having anything at all to show for the cost and effort they have put in. When this happens and things go wrong, it is often actually not the student's fault. The root cause can often lie in poor supervision, poor institutional support, unclear objectives, communication issues between student and supervisor, and so on. The purpose of this book is two-fold: to boost your confidence in pursuing higher study if this is something you want to do, and to help you avoid common pitfalls, to enable you to successfully complete your own rewarding PhD journey.

Let's first look at the issue of confidence. Starting a PhD can be daunting, and many students might initially feel overwhelmed and might not know where to start. Some students might not consider themselves capable of doing a PhD, although they very clearly are. For example, students who do not have anyone else in their family with an advanced degree, and students from Black and ethnic minority backgrounds, encounter obstacles to accessing higher education (more on this in Chapter 6). So, this book is intended to give you confidence in reaching for a PhD and to make the prospect less daunting. No student should be held back in their academic ambitions due to their background, race, gender, or other characteristics that have nothing to do with academic ability. If you are intrigued by the PhD process but currently lack confidence to embark on the journey, this book will boost your confidence.

It is important to acknowledge that a lack of confidence, although it can be overcome, is understandable. It is easy to conclude that you lack the ability to succeed in academia if there are no positive role models for you to aspire to: if there are no people in your family or your neighbourhood who have got a doctorate, if there are few or no people in a certain high-status field that look like you and that come from where you come from, it can be hard to have the confidence to enter that field, and to recognise your strengths and ability to succeed in it. If you can see no people among PhD holders who resemble you – physically, in terms of background, in terms of geographic origin – and if you believe people with PhDs come from affluent backgrounds and are mainly white and male, then it is no surprise you lack confidence if you happen to be something other than a middle-class, white male! But take courage: it is possible for you to succeed. Yes, there are still structural barriers for people from certain backgrounds and certain ethnic groups. Prejudice and discrimination are real, leading to unfair disadvantage for some. But there are people who are committed to change things for the better, and commitment to social justice is probably more prevalent in academia than in many other industries. This is a theme that emerged very strongly when I interviewed PhD students from minoritised backgrounds about their experiences: although many agreed that they faced additional obstacles at university due to their demographic background, they also emphasised that overall, they experienced academia and higher education as more accepting, supportive, and inclusive than other contexts they had encountered in their lives. More and more minoritised people succeed in obtaining a PhD, and they become agents of change themselves: as a minoritised person with a PhD, you can become a vital part of the struggle for a fairer world for all and become a role model for the next generation. So, if a lack of confidence prevents you from exploring PhD options: take courage. You can succeed, and you will succeed if you go about it the right way and make sure you benefit from a supportive context. Many of the subsequent chapters focus on what a supportive context looks like and how to ensure you seek, find, and co-create such sympathetic conditions.

Let's now come to the second point and reflect on the issue of pitfalls that make people trip up in their PhD journey. It is a crying shame when PhD students drop out, especially in those frequent cases where this is due to factors the student is not responsible for. By clearly explaining the process of doing a PhD and the contextual factors that lead to or prevent success, this book intends to give you invaluable insights into what to ask for, what to look out for, what to object to, what to request, and what to expect. A clear understanding of 'what good looks like' will enable you to see when you are not given the support you should expect and to troubleshoot accordingly. This will be especially useful for anyone who lacks the social networks and connections that might give other access to advice on how to succeed in a higher education environment: if you are from a minoritised background, this book will 'lift the curtain' and make crucial information available to all. The idea is to level the playing field, to make a PhD a viable option for everyone. Let's make sure failure is not your story: together we will navigate your way to PhD success.

## For whom will this book add value?

PhD programmes differ between subjects, universities, and countries, but they also all have features in common. Some aspects of the PhD journey are specific to a certain programme (e.g., admissions criteria), other aspects will be universally true for all PhD programmes (e.g., the importance of navigating the student-supervisor relationship with skill). Most chapters of this book address universally shared principles and will be relevant to anyone considering a PhD, irrespective of subject area or country of study. The principles described in Chapter 2 are especially relevant for anyone interested in pursuing a PhD in the UK, especially in the social sciences, because these are the settings the author is most familiar with. But even for the issues described in Chapter 2, many of them will generalise from the social sciences to other subject areas and from the UK to other European countries and the USA. So, this book is relevant for anyone wanting to embark on a PhD journey, irrespective of topic, time, and place. This book provides useful insights for those already benefitting from a supportive background; it can supplement advice given from family members and friends. In particular though, this book aims to equalise access to higher education by making inside 'tips of the trade' available to all: to empower all prospective students with a sense of confidence. Knowledge on how to navigate your road to your doctor title should not be restricted to old boys' networks – let's make it available to everyone! To achieve this, this book will walk you through the process from applying for a place to successfully defending the thesis in a doctoral viva.

## A word on terminology – who has a 'minoritised background'?

Above, I have used the catch-all phrase 'minoritised background' to refer to PhD students who are in danger of facing additional barriers to, or during, their studies because of their demographic background. The accepted terminology to describe this group of students often changes over time, with terms that were accepted even relatively recently quickly becoming frowned upon. An example is the use of the term BAME in UK higher education, which stands for 'Black, Asian, and Minority Ethnic.' This was standard terminology from the 2000s onwards, but since the 2020s it has been criticised for lumping together diverse groups, masking vast differences in lived experience and educational barriers and attainment gaps. Without clearly describing where the problems with fair and equal access and support are, it is impossible to design solutions to the problems. The term BAME has also been criticised for centring around whiteness as the default. There is no clear, universally accepted substitute for the BAME label at present, but the prevailing trend is to instead talk about 'ethnic minorities' or 'people from ethnic minority backgrounds', and to focus the data analysis (e.g., when looking at achievement gaps) on specific ethnic groups, rather than an overall global label to avoid overseeing important between-group nuances.

An additional concern about the term BAME that I would add is that although it is clearly of pivotal importance to consider fairness through an ethnic lens, it is also important to consider other kinds of obstacles. People can face challenges on the basis of many personal characteristics, for example gender (the 'leaky pipeline' problem in higher education being a clear illustration of this), religion (e.g., with prejudice against Jewish and Muslim students being a very live issue on British campuses right now), sexual orientation (e.g., with prejudice against members of the LGBTQ+ community posing challenges), and socioeconomic status (SES) or social class (e.g., with those from non-middle or upper class backgrounds often being 'first generation' at university within their families).

To avoid the term BAME, I use 'minoritised background.' I prefer this to 'people from ethnic minority backgrounds', because the term 'minoritised' nicely captures the notion of being at the receiving end of someone else's perceptions and prejudice: minoritised people are not inherently disadvantaged because of the way they are, they are disadvantaged because of the way they are treated by others – it is something that is 'done' to the person at the receiving end. It shifts the focus from inherent characteristics to systems of power. It acknowledges that students are made into minorities by structural processes (e.g., racism, colonialism), not because they are numerically fewer. However, terminology is often deeply contested, and while I quite like the term, it can be criticised for casting minority members in a passive victim role, thereby denying them agency. On the plus side, talking about 'minoritised people' allows widening the scope beyond ethnicity and including those facing challenges on the basis of their gender, religion, sexual orientation, social class, disability, or other characteristics. This is another reason why I quite like the term.

I also sometimes use the term 'global majority.' It aptly captures the fact that those traditionally in power, in particular white, middle-class men, are a minority in the global context. White, middle-class men are massively outnumbered globally by humans that do not meet this description. This throws into sharp relief the unfairness inherent in our educational systems, where much power rests in the hands of just a few, not on the basis of their greater merit but on the basis of their good fortune, having been born as a certain person. However, this term too can be criticised – if BAME is criticised for overgeneralising across different diverse groups, this is true even more so for 'global majority'! Moreover, I have yet to meet a PhD student who faces additional challenges because of their demographic background who would profess to identify with the 'global majority.' As a social psychologist interested in social group identity, I am acutely aware that often the best way to describe people is to accept and honour the ways in which those people describe themselves. How valuable, then, is the term global majority, if no one actually sees themselves as a global majority member?

Overall, my approach will be that where a catch-all term is needed to describe those who face obstacles because of their demographic background, I will use the term 'minoritised' or 'global majority.' But, when it comes to understanding lived experience and addressing challenges faced by specific sub-sections of the population, it is usually advantageous to be much more fine-grained and look at different subgroups separately to avoid masking and missing major differences.

One issue that must be acknowledged is that often discussions about unfairness in higher education invite competitive victimhood claims between different groups. The question of who faces the most discrimination can be hotly debated: are the greatest obstacles put in the way of bright, promising students because of their race or ethnicity, their gender, their socioeconomic background and class, their disability, sexual orientation, gender identity, age, nationality/immigration status, accent, caring responsibilities? Or the intersectionality between several of those characteristics, and if so, which exactly? I will make no value judgement on this question here. This book intends to remove barriers for all prospective students who face challenges, no matter how large or small those challenges are compared to someone else with a different demographic background.

## Top tips

1 Reflect on why you are interested in doing a PhD – is the goal an academic career, or a leg up in the job market outside of academia? The end goal might well inform your choices along the way (more on this in Chapter 8), although it is also not uncommon for people to change their minds about their post-PhD goals during the PhD process!

2 Research thoroughly what the PhD programme you are considering entails. This detail should be available on the universities' websites but if information is missing or unclear, consider emailing the relevant PGR (Post Graduate Research) Lead in the department you are interested in, or a prospective PhD supervisor who works in the field in which you are interested. Will the programme run over three or four years? How much classroom-based teaching does it entail, and how much of the work consists of independent study? Do they accept self-funded students, or only those with a scholarship? What opportunities do they offer in terms of studentships and in terms of earning a living, for example by working as a teaching or research assistant during your studies?

3 If you are a first-generation student (meaning that no one else in your family has been to university or completed a PhD), and if you belong to a group that has historically been discriminated against, please realise you belong in academia! You are especially needed in academia! Discrimination should not be a barrier to anyone who wants to do a PhD.

4 If things go wrong during your PhD, keep in mind that the problem does not necessarily lie with you. Are you supported in the right way? Are there things that can be improved in the context to enable you to work better? Be aware of the impact of contextual factors on your ability to succeed, and don't be afraid to demand improvements if support is found to be lacking.

# 2 Finding the key to the door

## Your way in

### You don't need to be Einstein

It is my firm belief that most people of at least average academic ability can do a PhD. You really do not need to be Einstein to succeed. Many people assume that those who do a PhD must have an IQ that is off the scale and that this achievement is out of their own reach, because of an unfounded lack in confidence in their own academic abilities. I have several non-academic friends who seem to believe that I must be super smart, purely on account of the fact that I have a PhD. While this is amusing to me to some extent, it is also worrying: people who wrongly believe a goal to be out of their reach because they mistakenly feel they lack some innate ability to reach it will not attempt to attain that goal and will limit their own options.

In addition to a lack of self-esteem and trust in their own abilities, there is another barrier that many people face in being admitted to a PhD programme: they don't know how to go about applying, they don't know what potential supervisors look for, and they have a limited understanding of the admissions process. This is where this book can help.

### The admissions process – prior degree requirements

First and foremost, to start a PhD you will need an undergraduate degree. Depending on your subject, this will either be a BSc or a BA. Often, it is helpful if this degree is in the same subject area as that of your PhD, although this is not always strictly required. Especially in the social sciences and humanities, a prior degree in a related area can be perceived as sufficient. Typically, in the UK you need to have obtained at least a 2.1 (60% average or above in your undergraduate degree) to be admitted, although this requirement varies between different institutions. A performance at undergraduate level between 50% and 59% on average will result in a 2:2 and is often not considered a sufficient basis for higher study. If your undergraduate degree is not from the UK, then admissions teams will convert it to the UK equivalent to see if you meet the requirements.

DOI: 10.4324/9781003630074-2

This is often not an exact science: when I came to the UK as an MSc student, I was initially rejected by the admissions team on the basis of my prior qualification – I appealed and my appeal was upheld (with the help of a UK academic at that institution who I had got on side and who backed me up against the admissions team). I ended up graduating with a high mark, confirming that a revision to the original admissions decision was sensible. The take-home message here is that it might be worth challenging the decision of admissions officers if you are convinced of the strength of your credentials. Equally, as a prospective PhD student you should not necessarily take at face value what universities say about their admissions criteria: sometimes requirements can be a bit laxer than what published criteria would suggest. After all, if there are spare places, the university will look to fill those spaces, and if the pool of applicants is unexpectedly weaker in a certain year, requirements might well be interpreted more loosely. Having said this, many of the more prestigious institutions will have many more applications than places, and competition for places will hence be fierce. Here, a 2.1 degree will often not be enough; you will need to have obtained a strong 'first class' degree (70% average or above) to be competitive.

Occasionally, a student who did not manage to achieve a 2:1 for their undergraduate degree sets their heart on doing a PhD. Maybe 'life happened' during their undergraduate studies and personal events prevented the student from performing at their absolute best. Moreover, some students only 'blossom' academically later in life. It is, of course, a shame when a period of questionable choices and of partying rather than studying in one's early 20s curbs one's ability to follow a dream for further study that only arises later in life. For such students, doing a Master's degree before the PhD can be an entry route. Master's degrees are usually (although not always) Postgraduate Taught Programmes (as opposed to Research Programmes), with a strong emphasis on classroom teaching and learning. Depending on the PhD programme of interest, most admissions tutors will look for at least a 'Merit' result in the MSc/MA (60% average or above), although realistically for competitive programmes at least a Distinction (70% or above) will be required in order to be a competitive PhD candidate.

Many PhD students first complete a Master's degree even if they have excellent undergraduate results, and the experience of a Master's is typically regarded as an immensely helpful foundation and basis that makes tackling PhD work easier. However, the completion of a Master's is not strictly required, and some students do move to PhD straight after their undergraduate degree. In terms of admissions criteria, many universities will look at the performance in the last academic qualification, and this can compensate for prior mishaps. Being admitted to a PhD programme with a 'Distinction' at MSc/MA level but only a 2:2 at undergraduate level can be a realistic option.

Although the degree results are the most important criterion for admission to a PhD programme, there are other achievements and credentials that can help boost your profile. Prospective supervisors look for evidence of strong academic aptitude, drive, and prior training. If you are already thinking about a PhD path during your undergraduate studies, there are some things you can work towards early on to enhance your CV. Experience working with an academic as a paid or unpaid research assistant during your undergraduate studies will boost your profile. I know of many students who obtained such a post simply by proactively approaching different academics and communicating that they are keen on this experience. Presenting your work at academic conferences and events will be an asset. One of my PhD students presented her work at a PGR convention when she was still a Master's student, demonstrating initiative and academic excellence early on. Last but not least, already having co-authored peer-reviewed publications when applying for funding will make you a very strong candidate. If your degree includes a final year project, as psychology degrees for example do, talk to your supervisor about your ambitions to publish the work. If you are working in someone's lab, ask the lead academic if there are opportunities to get involved with publications. Remember, there are no stupid questions, and if you seem keen and ambitious, this is likely to reflect very positively on how you will be perceived.

## The admissions process for international students

If you are an international student looking to study at a British or US university, those universities will have admissions teams whose job it is to 'translate' results obtained abroad in different education systems into the home system. If you have performed very well in your home country, and if the institution you attended is reputable, you will be given a high score and be admitted.

In addition, if English was not your language of instruction, most universities will require a certificate confirming sufficient proficiency. The most commonly used tests that are widely accepted are IELTS and TOEFL. Generally speaking, you don't have to be super advanced to pass this requirement, but a reasonable level of competence is required in order to obtain an acceptable test result. Language test requirements might differ between different universities and different courses, so if this is a concern it might pay off to shop around.

## Agents, visas, transnational education, and employment

A lot of international students use agents to guide them through the admissions process. This is true for prospective students interested in undergraduate study, but also postgraduate study. Agents will start by understanding the student's career goals and degree expectations, and they might recommend different universities to the student. They will help the student understand the entry requirements and provide support in preparing the application and then dealing with any follow-up, for example if an offer for a place is made that is conditional on the supply of further documents or information. Agents also provide support to prospective students for obtaining visas. Upon acceptance at a university, international students are issued a Confirmation of Acceptance for Studies (CAS), which is needed to apply for a UK student visa. Some agents also provide pre-departure workshops and support sessions, for example focused on cultural adjustment tips. All of these services usually come at a substantial cost.

Is it value for money to employ an agent to provide these support services? Should you be looking to do this? The answer to this question depends on your situation and priorities. Usually, agents do not have information that would not also be accessible to you directly. A lot of universities have a wealth of information on their websites on all relevant aspects of transnational education. You could save money and do the research yourself. What this would cost you is considerable time – digesting complex information from lots of diverse sources is time-intensive. In addition, for PhD-level study, agents are not well placed to advise on a choice of supervisor. Only you can know which academic profile matches your interests most closely, and prospective supervisors would mostly be taken aback by being contacted via an agent, rather than the prospective student themselves.

When talking to international students who have come to the UK, the main reason they cite for having used an agent is, to put it bluntly, fear of being rejected for the visa. A visa application is high stakes: if you are refused a visa, in many countries you will be asked to declare this in future visa applications. Making a mistake in the visa application that could be a reason for a rejection is synonymous for many aspiring students with messing up their future prospects. They are therefore willing to pay a hefty financial price for peace of mind in relation to their visa application in particular. Given the price of making a mistake, this might be a sound and sensible investment for you. However, there is nothing inherent in the visa and university admissions process that means that an educated, intelligent prospective student would not be able to navigate the process under their own steam. Many universities attend education fairs in international locations, either by sending their own international recruitment staff there or via agents they are partnering with. It is perfectly possible to find your dream institution by attending fairs and doing your own research online – an agent's recommendation on choice of institution can help, but it is not essential.

As with any service, there can be huge quality differences between different providers. Some are simply not that competent, responsive, reliable, or trustworthy. Reputation and evidence of past success matter when selecting an agent. Many British universities also authorise and train specific agents to represent them in specific countries. Finding an agent via this set-up requires you to make a clear choice on the institution you are interested in and to find an agent who is authorised to represent that university. This has the advantage that you can be confident that the agent is not a rogue operator. A further advantage is that then often the service is free to you because the university typically pays the agent commission for the student's successful enrolment. In sum, there are advantages to using a trusted agent as well as disadvantages. However, you should make sure that you do your research and under no circumstances sign up with a dud service provider. It is important to be clear about the agents' reputation and the exact service they will provide to you.

This chapter is about finding your route to your PhD programme, but in order to decide where to apply to, many international students have a keen eye on where they want their studies to lead to and on their post-study career goals. Frequently used buzz words are 'value for money' and 'return on investment' – students want to know that they will make up the outlay they've had to pay for their education with substantially enhanced earning potential post-study. It can be quite obscure and hard to determine what the 'return on investment' is for different degree programmes from different universities. This does not necessarily mean that the return on investment isn't large – it just means that the information is hard to find. Your prospective supervisor is unlikely to help with this also: academics are trained in teaching their subject matter, not on how best to turn this training into industry salaries. However, many universities do publish on their websites statistics about post-study employment rates and about typical careers graduates go into and typical companies graduates work at. They might also showcase alumni, to illustrate the illustrious careers graduates have built on the back of their degree. Researching this information can give you an idea of where the degree might lead you.

One question at the fore of many international students' minds is whether there is an option to stay in the country post-degree and seek employment there. Researching this aspect is also difficult because visa and immigration rules frequently change. For example, in the UK at the time of writing it is possible to obtain a post-study visa for up to two years. In this time, an international applicant would need to find an employer who wants to sponsor them via a Certificate of Sponsorship (CoS) in order to stay beyond the two years. However, the rules and relevant timeframes are under constant review, so there is no guarantee that the process will still be the same at the point where you are applying for your place! The central take-home message from this is: in order to decide whether to apply for a place at a certain institution or to work with a certain person, it is valuable to think about your end goal and to be as clued up as possible about the later career opportunities and legislative context that might shape your next steps post-PhD. Chapter 7 discusses in more detail other issues relevant to international students specifically.

## Finding funding: scholarship opportunities

Many universities will appraise prospective applicants in relation to two questions: first, is this candidate strong enough to complete the PhD programme and should they be admitted onto the programme? And second, is this candidate so promising that they are worthy of university funding? The criteria applied to both questions differ. There are usually more places for PhD supervision than there are funded studentships. Consequently, a weaker academic profile might be sufficient for being offered a place, but not sufficient for securing funding.

Being offered a scholarship by a university is not only a sign of confidence in your academic abilities, but it also takes the pressure off having to find other means of supporting yourself during your studies. In some cases, such scholarships come with an obligation to contribute to undergraduate teaching (be clear on the hours that are expected). Although clearly it is nice to receive a scholarship that typically covers not only tuition fees but also a monthly stipend for living expenses, in reality those scholarships tend not to be very generous. Usually, they do not allow for a more extravagant lifestyle than that of a typical undergraduate student, at least in the UK – funding in some other European countries is more generous. PhD students therefore tend to be comparatively 'poor.' The trade-off is, of course, that upon successful completion of a PhD you are likely to have significantly improved your earning potential and prospects on the job market in the future. But this comes at the cost of some years of relative financial hardship. Especially for mature students who might already have gotten used to a certain lifestyle and financial security, this might be a rather off-putting prospect and ought to be thought through quite carefully.

Another key point to be aware of is that universities in the UK get penalised, in terms of reputation damage, for PhD students who do not complete their degree within the allocated time. This makes many institutions quite twitchy about admitting students who are perceived to be 'high risk,' for example because of a mediocre academic track record or weaker English language skills. One factor that is known to put students at risk of non-completion is the need to self-fund their studies. Students who do not benefit from a full studentship often have to work evening shifts in second jobs to support themselves during their degree, and this added stress and time commitment unsurprisingly can have a detrimental effect on 'completion' rates, i.e., whether students actually manage to successfully graduate.

For this reason, some universities or departments do not allow self-funded students; they only admit those students who they have agreed to support with a scholarship or those students who can provide clear evidence of having studentship support from another source, for example the government of their home country. If you do not have your own studentship, it is important to ask questions of your chosen institution and to gain clarity about its criteria for admission to the programme, its criteria for providing funding, and whether it does or does not take self-funded students.

Those looking for a PhD scholarship can explore different potential sources of support: universities themselves usually reserve part of their own budget to fund promising PhD students and advertise scholarships on their websites, but there are other sources of financial support. Different charities might also support PhD students interested in advancing knowledge in an area within the charity's remit.

In the UK, PhD students can also apply to obtain government funding, administered through Research Councils. At present, government funding for PhD-level study in the UK is administered via UKRI and universities that are part of Doctoral Training Partnerships (DTPs) and Centres for Doctoral Training (CDTs). In DTPs, universities form partnerships funded by a Research Council to support cohorts of PhD students across multiple disciplines within the council's remit. In CDTs, training is provided through focused, often interdisciplinary programmes providing structured training in specific research areas. Applicants for funding via these avenues often go through a multi-step application process which can involve selection at departmental, institutional, and finally overall network level, and across different disciplines, so there are multiple stages at which the proposal must succeed in order to obtain funding, and the required standard of applicants is therefore very high. The application process can often be a bit opaque and confusing for applicants, and the best person to provide guidance is your supervisor (once you have persuaded them that they want to champion you and work with you). UKRI DTPs also offer funding for international students, although the proportion earmarked for this is quite small, so in some ways the competition for international students via this funding route is even stiffer.

Many international governments also support students wanting to study in the UK or the USA, often with a stipulation that scholarship recipients need to then return home to teach and 'pay back' the investment, at least for a certain length of time. If you want to be able to focus on your studies and give yourself the best chances of succeeding, a scholarship from one of these sources is extremely helpful, even though money on these scholarships is usually still tight. The best person to ask whether your chosen programme accepts self-funders, and what scholarship opportunities might be available, is the person you hope to be supervised by. More on the pivotal importance of your relationship with your prospective supervisor will be covered below in this chapter and also in Chapter 4.

## Finding your topic

A PhD takes typically 3–4 years of concentrated work. Much of this work is self-directed, which means that you as a student have to motivate yourself (which can be a job in its own right for procrastinators), set your own goals, and make sure that the work gets done. This type of project can only succeed if you are inherently interested in the topic you are working on. Having the self-discipline to drive something forward that bores you senseless would be too much to ask of even the most diligent character. Essentially, unless you are passionate about your chosen question, topic, or line of enquiry, there seems little point devoting three years of your life to it.

Having said this, it is not a requirement to be obsessively fascinated by your chosen topic either. Some PhD students are more moderate in their passion than others. As a PhD student and academic, I have certainly met peers who believe that their topic is the most exciting and important thing in the world, but I have also met others who quite like their work, but at the end of the day its importance pales against the importance of favourite hobbies, other interests, or family connections. I myself certainly have a limit to how much time I am willing to sacrifice for doing my research when the alternative could be spending time with my children. An important question to ask yourself is this: would working on this topic excite me more than other things I could be doing with my working life, such as working for a charitable cause I believe in? Working in a sector where I can earn lots of money? If none of the alternatives seem more appealing than the PhD research, then this is a solid foundation for embarking on this particular adventure.

## Finding your supervisor

The quest for the right supervisor and the quest for the right topic are intertwined and strongly related. Academics are highly specialised, and you need to find a person who is able to supervise your chosen topic. Your choice of topic defines the pool of potential supervisors, and your chosen supervisor defines the range of questions you can study under their guidance. When you have a rough idea of which area of research interests you, google the topic and see what institutions, research papers, and potential supervisors come up. Study the people highlighted in your search carefully before selecting a handful whom you will approach by email with a preliminary enquiry as to whether they could consider taking you on as a PhD student.

An interesting question is how many PhD students your potential supervisor has already supervised to completion. A track record of successful supervision tells you a lot. At the same time, sometimes more junior supervisors can be more diligent and less jaded – at the end of the day, the person has to 'feel' right. Entering a supervision agreement with someone you haven't researched is like 'Marriage at first sight': you are buying a pig in a poke. Make sure you have a conversation with your potential supervisor before committing, ideally face-to-face or mediated by Teams/Zoom/WhatsApp/Skype. Another informative conversation you could have is with former students of the person you are considering working with: what do they have to say about their experiences? When students approach when students approach me who I am interested in taking on, I often put them in touch with former students of mine for a chat (I trust they will say good things about me). The key message is: vet your potential supervisor carefully. It is hard to overstate how important your relationship with your supervisor is. In German, a PhD supervisor is called a 'Doctor Father' although with women thankfully now being more strongly represented among the highly skilled workforce there are also, of course, many 'Doctor Mothers.' Either way, the term nicely conveys that your supervisor should guide you, advise you, nurture, and support you on your way to independence in your scientific scholarship.

Working with a supportive, knowledgeable person is at least as important as choosing a topic you won't get bored with, so there can sometimes be a need for a trade-off to be made: do you work with this great person who comes highly recommended but whose specialisation isn't exactly in your core interest area, or do you work with a person who has a reputation for being grumpy and unavailable but who is interested in exactly the same things you are? Your search might unearth that there are different people who seem to be a more or less good fit with you, given your interests, and that those people are based at more or less strong institutions, or more or less strong schools (also sometimes called departments). You might also find yourself wondering: is it better to go with a great supervisor who is based at a mediocre institution, or is it better to go with a mediocre supervisor based at a great institution? More on trade-offs related to supervisor choice will be covered in Chapter 4. Finding the right supervisor is one of the most important make-or-break tasks of completing a PhD. It is estimated that only 40–50% of students who begin PhD programmes complete their degrees, and I firmly believe that for those cases who fail, the lion's share of blame can often be put squarely at the supervisor's door. Don't shy away from asking prospective supervisors about their student completion rates. This, as well as your sense of how supportive of and invested in their students' success they are, can be an important piece of evidence in your decision making.

## Finding your university

I talked about 'finding your supervisor' first before talking about searching for the right institution, because in many ways I believe the supervisor is more important than the institution. If you are working with an amazing person in a less-well known institution, you are likely to have a wonderful time; if you are working with a difficult supervisor in a famous institution, you are likely to be miserable.

Having said all this, it is important to be aware of the overall institutional reputation, which is often correlated with how well the institution is resourced, how well it is run, and how easy it is to work in it. For example, in the UK there are different groupings of institutions that can be informative. There is a prestigious 'Russell Group' of universities, and members of this group are generally considered to be very desirable destinations for study. There is also an important distinction between Pre- and Post-92 universities. Post-92 universities are institutions that were polytechnics rather than universities before 1992, at which point they gained the status of universities. In higher education, there can be a bit of snobbery against Post-92 universities which tend to be focused more on teaching and vocational training delivery than on basic research. Having said this, some Post-92 institutions are truly excellent. The 'feel' of Pre- and Post-92 universities can be quite different from each other. Before you commit to a place, make sure you inform yourself about what kind of institution you are dealing with. One source of information for this is university league tables.

## How informative are league tables?

In the UK and the USA, institutional league tables are taken extremely seriously. Many of the most influential league tables are produced once a year. For example, in the UK the Complete University Guide and the *Guardian* are rankings that students consult when deciding where to study for their degree. Institutional rankings can vary in different tables, with the same institution doing significantly better in one table compared to another. Rankings can also change year-on-year. There is often truly little variation in terms of which universities are ranked at the top and are considered to be the best. The reputational advantage of top-ranking universities is often matched by the quality of their students and the resources these institutions have at their disposal. Your peers at these places will often have more impressive CVs, seem smarter, and the built environment and support for your research might be much higher quality. There is also often stability in terms of which unfortunate institutions find themselves at the bottom. In contrast, there can be a lot of movement in the 'middle' between years or newspapers. Consequently, although it is true that it often means a great deal whether an institution ranks towards the top of the league table or towards the bottom, there is a lot of 'noise' in the middle. Often, a university that is ranked 30th will not necessarily be materially qualitatively better than a university ranked 40th in any discernible or noticeable way.

To complicate matters further, in the UK, league tables are produced not only for institutions overall, but also for different subject units which are usually called 'schools' or 'departments.' Hence, you can consider not only the ranking of the institution/university overall, but also the ranking for the specific subject you are interested in. If this is not complex and confusing enough, there are also several types of performance indicators. There are metrics and league tables indicating teaching quality, learning environment, and educational and professional outcomes achieved by students (TEF results), as well as research quality results (Research Excellence Framework (REF). There is also an important metric indicating overall student satisfaction National Student Satisfaction Survey (NSS) results.

Often, your chosen institution can appear in a vastly different light, depending what metric you consult. For example, I am based at a university which tends to rank towards the middle of the league tables in institutional terms, but which is currently third in terms of research quality for my subject, psychology, jointly with Oxford. Last year, the NSS results for my department were good; this year, they are outstanding. A confused prospective student might ask: which league table is the most relevant one? Which one matters more, the institutional ranking or the subject ranking?

Interestingly, the obsession with institutional league tables is particularly prevalent in the Anglophone world. In some other top academic destinations such as Germany, the differences between universities in terms of prestige and resources are a lot less pronounced than in the UK or the USA – higher education in some countries is much more of a level playing field. In France, there is widely shared cultural knowledge that certain universities are the most prestigious (e.g., the Sorbonne), but this is not confirmed or reassessed on a yearly basis by conducting a massive exercise of rating and ranking. League tables for French and German universities do exist, but they are typically produced by English-speaking sources. What we end up with is a system where the Anglophone world is trying to rank higher education providers in other countries, with the natives of those countries finding the idea of doing this often rather bewildering.

Taking all this into account, which rankings should you consider when trying to decide on an institution? Generally, as a PhD student you should be more interested in research-relevant indicators than in teaching-relevant indicators, so the REF score is more meaningful for you than the NSS score. As a PhD student, you will be part of the research community, so research performance is often more diagnostic. In terms of whether to look at subject/department-level outcomes or at institution/university-level ratings, the answer to what matters most depends to no small extent on whether you want to stay in academia or not. If you are planning to leave academia upon completion of your PhD, having a degree from a top-ranking university such as Oxford or Cambridge will give you a strong competitive advantage – the prestige associated with some of the old names is not to be underestimated. The same is true for the top-ranking universities in the USA, such as Yale, Harvard, or Stanford. If you are planning to stay in academia, the subject-level indicators are often more meaningful than the institutional indicators. Experts in the field will know that a certain department at a famous university is actually not that good in a certain area, or that there is a centre of excellence in a certain subject in a less-well known institution. If the person you want to impress is an expert in your PhD subject (e.g., if they are an expert on a recruitment panel judging your job application for a Lectureship/Assistant Professorship at a university), they will by definition know a lot about the subject and the higher education market related to it, and more specific subject/department-level information will be most meaningful to them. If the person you want to impress knows little about your PhD subject (e.g., if they are a recruitment panel member in a different industry outside academia), higher-level indicators such as the overall reputation of the institution from which you graduated will be more meaningful to them.

## Your initial approach to the supervisor: the first email

So, you have identified some people who share your interests and could be potential supervisors, and you have decided that they are based at an institution you are interested in. You also believe that you might meet the admissions criteria – you have a strong undergraduate degree result and are reasonably proficient in the language. You might not know exactly what score is required on your language certificate yet, but your potential supervisor might be able to advise further on this once you have established a relationship with them. Where do you go from here?

Some students take all their certificates and documents and submit them to the admissions department of the university. This is what you would do if you wanted to do an undergraduate degree or a Master's, but doing this for a PhD application would be a mistake. In order to get your foot in the door for a PhD place, you are best advised to contact the prospective supervisor directly – email them! And, if they are interested, schedule a follow-up meeting with them to explore this further.

There are a number of key pieces of information supervisors will look for in your initial email. Most importantly, the supervisor will want to know that you are interested in questions that match their own programme of research, but that you also have the capacity to be an independent thinker. Customise the email to communicate that you have researched the supervisor and that you know what their research interests are. The supervisor wants to know that they were not contacted randomly, but that you specifically picked them because of their expertise and reputation. Most supervisors will also want to see that you are not interested in simply 'cloning' what they have already done, but that you have the potential to go beyond it. For this reason, it is a good idea to include a preliminary 1–2 page research proposal of what you hope to study in your PhD. Don't present this as set in stone; the supervisor may want to mould and improve it; but do put something on paper that can be a starting point for the two of you to work on together. Supervisors also differ on how happy they are to supervise outside their core area. Some have rather narrow interests and want all their students to stick quite closely to a specific narrow research area; others are more adventurous and are more comfortable supervising more widely outside their core area. The content of your proposal will differ for different academic subjects; in the social sciences what supervisors will look for is not only an outline of research ideas, hypotheses, and questions, but also an indication of your methodological approach.

The supervisor will also want to know that you meet the entry requirements. If you have an excellent undergraduate degree result, mention this and include evidence. If you have successfully passed a language proficiency test, mention this and include evidence.

There are other pieces of information that might be relevant and that you might want to share. Have you got significant work experience already that marks you out as someone who is mature and able to deliver? Have you got work experience as a research assistant in someone's lab during your undergraduate, have you presented your work at any conferences, have you co-authored any peer-reviewed publications already? Have you got lived experience in the subject in which you are interested? Do you have networks (e.g., with industry) that might be of benefit to the work you are proposing to carry out? Consider what might make you attractive to the supervisor. If you do not have any such attributes, don't despair; they are not essential. But if you do have them, you might as well flaunt them.

If you have already obtained PhD funding, maybe through a charity or government scholarship, absolutely mention it. If you do not have funding yet, ask intelligent questions about what funding might be available. The supervisor will be able to advise on university scholarships or schemes you could potentially apply for together. If you manage to convince someone that they want to work with you, you've cleared the first and possibly most difficult hurdle already. Some departments allocate PhD studentships to specific members of staff, so if you strike gold, you may have contacted someone who has been allocated funding and is currently looking to recruit. The flipside of this is, of course, that you might hit on the perfect supervisor who unfortunately has been taken off the scholarship allocation rota for the year in which you want to apply.

Researching potential supervisors and drafting customised emails is a significant amount of work. But, because of the many factors that might prevent an academic from wanting to take you on (e.g., lack of funding that particular year, or already being at capacity with a big group of existing PhD students), it is important that you don't put all eggs in one basket. Make several approaches; there will be more than one person in more than one institution that could potentially be a good fit for you.

## Top tips

1 Most people of at least average academic ability are able to complete a PhD. Don't assume that you are not clever enough. If you want it, go and get it.
2 Be clear on admissions criteria and make sure you meet them, for example by studying a bit more before taking a language proficiency test, or by completing an MSc if you flunked your undergraduate degree.
3 If you are an international student, consider whether or not to use an agent, and make sure you are clued up about future employment opportunities inside the country of study and your home country.
4 Research potential sources of funding and try to obtain a scholarship if possible. Be aware of trying to self-fund your studies without scholarship support: it is possible, but it is hard and hazardous.
5 Do your research to find some supervisors at institutions that would be an excellent fit for you and write a compelling and persuasive approach email that ensures that you get buy-in from the potential supervisor. Once you have hooked a potential supervisor they will be on your side and can provide further essential information on the admissions process, funding opportunities, and on how to ensure your proposal is as strong as possible. Once the supervisor wants to work with you, your application becomes their application too, and they will be motivated to get you through the door.

# 3 In the thick of it

## Managing your work and time

### Procrastination, pre-deadline panics, nagging guilt, and never being 'off'

One of the greatest joys and luxuries of doing a PhD can also be a curse: there are few jobs you could have where you'd have equal control over your time. Although your supervisor is meant to guide you on setting objectives, defining your deliverables, and helping you work out an appropriate timeline, in reality prevalent norms in UK academia mean that this supervision and guidance will only provide the loosest of structures. Unlike in an office job, there will be no one to check that you are at your desk at 9am, no one to check that your lunch break was not too long, and no one to check that you did any work at all last Friday, or last week, for that matter. There is the odd exception to this – some lab-based work might be time sensitive, for example, and if an experiment stalls because you didn't turn up as agreed, this will be noted. In the sciences, people tend to work more in teams, and colleagues might be reliant on you turning up, so there will be somewhat more 'social control' of your movements. In contrast, in the social sciences and humanities in particular, many scholars work in more solitary ways, and your schedule is likely to be entirely up to you to a considerable extent. For the most part, then, the task of managing your own workload will be mainly up to you, the PhD student.

Although some students find this liberating, others really struggle. All too often, deadlines (e.g., for an upgrade or for a conference paper submission) are ignored for the longest time – the beach beckons, or the park, or the pub. Even cleaning the windows and deep cleaning the fridge can be tempting pursuits for the procrastinator trying to find reasons not to sit down at the desk to tackle the most important task. Then, the night before the deadline, students find themselves pulling all-nighters and trying to make up for lost time. The habits acquired during undergraduate study are often also indulged when later pursuing a PhD.

DOI: 10.4324/9781003630074-3

A tendency to procrastinate is the cause of a substantial proportion of stress associated with completing a PhD. Leaving things until the last minute, to a point when it starts to seem questionable whether lost time can be made up double-quick, is panic-inducing and bad for blood pressure, cortisol levels, and mental health (more on mental health in Chapter 5). Trying to cram an impossibly large amount of work into an exceedingly small portion of time will inevitably cause spikes of stress.

Moreover, students who play hooky rarely do so with a completely clear conscience. Whilst you are sitting in the sun having a drink with friends, there is this nagging feeling of guilt in the background and this little gremlin whispering in your ear saying: 'You should be working right now!' As a result, you might engage in a lot of alleged downtime and 'play' that is not truly relaxing because of your underlying bad conscience that keeps knocking. Many PhD students complain about constant low-level nagging guilt when they are not working and never feeling that they can be truly 'off.' This is exacerbated by being embedded in a culture which suggests that your work should be your passion, and your entire life, and you should work on your chosen topic with tireless dedication. Many academics see their work as their calling and their raison d'être. This rubs off on PhD students, who internalise the idea that they should be so dedicated to their work that they devote unlimited amounts of time to it. Some do and start working round the clock seven days a week. Others do not and instead turn into procrastinators but suffer from underlying feelings of constant guilt. Both the super-conscientious and the procrastinating students have in common that they rarely have proper downtime; they are either working or feeling that they should be working.

This is problematic because lots of research shows that in order to achieve maximum efficiency, it is absolutely essential to regularly 'switch off.' Short spurts of focused work, punctuated by true downtime and complete disengagement from work, typically lead to higher levels of productivity than long hours alone. The evidence points to the fact that people are not actually more productive the longer they work, and that shorter hours and proper time for switching off typically produce much higher productivity rates than long hours without the opportunity to recharge.

As a PhD student, please don't fall into this trap. One of the most useful pieces of advice I got from my own supervisor during my PhD was to never work on the weekends. His intervention came about six months into my PhD, after a period of time where I had worked so intensely, without proper time off, that I found myself getting close to burnout. My supervisor suggested I should treat my PhD just like any other job: turn up and work at the office 9–5 every day during the week and take evenings and weekends off. My switching to this approach was essential to staying sane during my PhD journey. It is something that I still practice to this day: I hardly ever work on weekends, and I rarely feel guilty about not working. I tell this to all my PhD students and hope to be a positive role model in this regard. We must not make it harder for ourselves than it needs to be. Feeling guilty about not working, whilst not working, is a waste of time, as you are neither being productive nor enjoying yourself. Let's eliminate work-related guilt from your life.

## Work-life balance: what is that?

Many academics are terrible at maintaining a healthy or even just reasonable work-life balance, and they inadvertently socialise their PhD students to develop the same dysfunction. As a student, hard as it is, resist! Your supervisor is not always right, and when they role-model unhelpful behaviour, you can choose a different path. Above, I advocate treating your PhD work like any other job and aiming for 9–5. In German there is a word for the time that you have off after having done your day's work: 'Feierabend.' It is different from leisure time, because it has connotations of having earned your free time because of work already completed. We all need more Feierabend periods in our lives.

Of course, a 9–5 will not suit everyone. This could, of course, also be a 12 noon to 8pm working day, or any other pattern that works for you, as long as there is a clear routine and delineation between work time and well-deserved off time. The beauty of academic flexibility is that you can choose your own regular pattern. Some people might have childcare issues that mean they need to take a break after the school pickup and then continue working after the children have gone to bed. Others might find that they are really unproductive in the afternoons and are best off starting super early and finishing before lunch. All these models are fine of course; there is no one size that fits all. You are best placed to work out which model suits you best.

Once you have figured out what works for you, however, stick to it. Treat it as a non-negotiable unless something really drastic happens. If you deviate from your routine too readily, you'll find that it quickly falls apart. One week it is sunny and you go off schedule to make the most of the nice weather, the next week your friend is moving and wants help Thursday morning, the next week your favourite TV show has some new episodes out and it seems very tempting to just have a little binge-watch before refocusing on your PhD. Your friends and family might also, once they realise that you are the master of your own time, start seeing you as someone who is always available to offer support or help whenever needed. You can easily see how too much flexibility around your routine can quickly jeopardise your long-term plans. Of course, rigidity needs to be applied with reason. I certainly did take some time away from my schedule occasionally when loved ones were unexpectedly in town, for example. But it is wise to consider such deviations carefully before embarking on them and to make conscious decisions before agreeing to changes to your pattern. Your routine is your friend: defend it.

## The benefits of structure: reduced cognitive load and greater goal commitment

There are some clear psychological benefits, as well as positive consequences for productivity, from having a predictable work schedule. Several studies focused on goal attainment have looked at factors that make it more likely that people stick to long-term goals, such as going to the gym regularly. This research clearly shows that making decisions is energy-sapping. Deciding between different options requires cognitive resources and mental energy. This is true even for relatively banal decisions, such as whether to have the lemon or blueberry muffin with your coffee: choice is exhausting. You can make your life slightly easier for yourself by eliminating some of the choice through pre-commitment and the formulation of a routine and plan you are committed to sticking to. If you have already decided that you will start work every Monday morning at 10am, you do not then need to wake up and agonise over whether you should really tackle your work that day or whether you should choose to put it off a little. Routines simplify our lives by reducing the cognitive load required for dealing with choice.

A related but slightly different mechanism relevant to the psychology of goal attainment is the beneficial effect of prior commitment to a goal. People are more likely to do something if they have previously already committed to it, compared to a situation where they are asked to decide for or against something on the spot. This is particularly true for slightly unpleasant tasks or those that require effort, such as going to the gym, sticking to a diet, or working on your PhD. People are more likely to execute a plan on Monday morning if they commit to the plan on Sunday evening, instead of leaving it until the last minute on Monday morning to decide how to proceed. Prior commitment is typically not needed if the goal is to encourage you to eat ice cream or have a glass of wine. In contrast, prior commitment can be absolutely crucial when it comes to ensuring that you tackle those tasks that we tend to procrastinate over. So, you can make a positive choice to make your life easier for yourself: commit to a regular work routine and take a load off your mind.

## Clearly defining the parameters: how much work do you have to do, and how much time do you have?

It is quite astonishing how many PhD students only have a sketchy understanding of the work they are expected to deliver and how tasks essential for producing the end product can be broken down and scheduled within the available time. To understand how to best tackle the to-do list, it is essential to be clear about those two parameters: what work are you expected to complete, and how much time do you have? Only once you are clear on those two factors are you able to work out how to schedule the work most effectively within the available time.

Often PhD students are afraid to ask their supervisor about the work that is expected, because they fear that they should know this already and do not want to advertise their ignorance. In this context, it is helpful to recall this universal truism: there is no such thing as a stupid question, the only thing that can be stupid is the answer. If you are not sure about what work you are expected to produce, ask. Ask your supervisor. Ask your advisor. Ask your peers. Ask about the word count, the number of studies, the typical number of references and citations, the typical standards. Do not stop at asking for guidance on what you are expected to produce, but try to generate an in-depth understanding by asking: what are the benchmarks? What criteria will be applied to judge the work? What is passable work? What does excellent work look like? I've often found that one of the best ways to understand the requirements of a PhD is to look at completed PhD theses in your discipline. These will give you a good idea what you are aiming for. Ideally, your supervisor will be able to provide you with a couple of theses from their previous students and contextualise those examples for you. Looking at excellent previous theses will give you a sense of 'what good looks like.' Only once you have a solid understanding of what a strong PhD thesis looks like will you be able to produce one. Do seek this guidance from your supervisor if you are confused about what is required of you. If you do not know what you are expected to produce and deliver, you will not be able to meet those ill-specified expectations.

## Break it down and monitor progress

Most students are thankfully clear on how much time they have available: in the UK, PhDs are typically expected to be completed within 3–4 years. Many scholarships and sources of funding will also last for this time only, although some avenues for support offer funding for longer (I have had several international students with funding from their home governments who were in this fortunate position). Whatever your timeframe, do discuss with your supervisor what you are both aiming for. On what date are you aiming to submit?

Once you know the end goal and the total time limit, the next job is to break the work down into sub-tasks. Working back from your target submission date, what are relevant milestones, intermediate goals, and what does an overall sensible project management plan look like? On the first day of your PhD registration period, the task you are faced with might appear insurmountably large. But it becomes manageable when broken down into bite-sized chunks. Don't think of the overall project that needs to be delivered, make a sensible plan and then work towards the next intermediate goal. This might be tackling your first empirical study only, writing the first ten pages of a literature review, or writing an outline of a chapter. Bit by bit, you will get the work done.

Make sure that you are working on a project timeline that your supervisor is on board with. If you and your supervisor have different timeframes in mind and this remains unspoken, this is likely to complicate matters unnecessarily. To have a clear and agreed plan, it is important that goals are concrete and SMART (specific, measurable, achievable, realistic, timely). So don't agree with your supervisor that you will aim to finish the next chapter 'soon'; be specific and agree that you will produce a certain number of words/pages by a concrete, specific date. Of course, sometimes our estimate of how long different tasks will take are not realistic, and in fact most people vastly underestimate how long things will take them. But having a concrete goal and date will give you something to aim for and monitor progress against.

In the context of monitoring progress, one important question is how often you should meet with your supervisor to benefit from their input and monitor progress. Common practices vary widely between different institutions and supervisors. There might still be one or two bad eggs who welcome their students onto the programme and then ask them to go away and hide in some dark corner of the library and not emerge until they have written the entire thesis virtually independently. This is clearly bad practice, and you deserve better. It would be reasonable to expect to see your supervisor for input at least once a month and more often than that when the work requires it.

In addition to an expectation that supervisors meet with their students regularly, many universities also have formal milestones of annual reviews and upgrades designed to monitor progress. During an annual review, a larger panel of colleagues might check that a student has made sufficient progress. An 'upgrade' is a formal process in the UK consisting of a viva voce that students need to pass, typically after about 1.5 years, before they even become 'proper' PhD students. Candidates admitted to PhD programmes are initially registered only to complete an MPhil, which is a lesser degree than a PhD. Only after passing their 'upgrade' do students become actual PhD students, so this is another significant milestone.

In terms of supervisory meetings along the way, my own practice is that I like to see my PhD students at least every two weeks. Some of these meetings will be long, others might just consist of a brief check in. I find regular meetings invaluable not only in order to monitor that everything stays on track, but also to check how the student is doing more broadly (see Chapter 5 on well-being). Too many PhD students struggle by themselves without support, whilst their supervisor is blissfully ignorant that anything is amiss. Over the typical course of a PhD, meeting frequency often declines. Very regular meetings are essential in the first year, and meeting regularity can then ease off in years 2 and 3 as the student learns to work increasingly independently, and as the project moves from the planning and execution phase into the write-up phase. Importantly, if you are not happy with how often you get to see your supervisor: say so. Your project is important, you are important, and it is your supervisor's job to give you the necessary attention. In sum, breaking down your large project into bite-sized chunks and having a concrete timeline with clearly specified sub-goals are key for successfully completing the project on time.

## Prioritising your tasks

One thing my students often tell me is that the work of a PhD student can feel overwhelming. There are so many things you should work on: the extensive literature review, the design of the first empirical study, the preparation of a class you have to teach, the journal club you need to prepare for, and so on. How should you go about deciding what to tackle first?

There are entire books dedicated to just this question. My students have found two tips especially helpful. The first recommendation is to follow the approach of the 'Three Ds': Diarise, Delegate, and Do. If there is a task that you cannot or do not want to do immediately, 'diarise' it: reserve a slot in your diary for it. By setting a specific time, you can ensure that it will get done, but you can also put it out of your mind for the time being to dedicate your mental energy to something else. If someone else can do the task for you, delegate. Unfortunately, PhD students do not often have the luxury to do this because they do not manage a team, but this might still be appropriate in certain situations. For example, you might be collaborating on a paper with a team of peers, and you could set clear expectations around how the division of labour should work. The 'Do' part is self-explanatory; these are the things you should tackle first without delay. But what tasks should fall into this category? Generally speaking, two types of tasks should find their way onto the 'Do' list: urgent tasks that are time sensitive. These tasks might have deadlines, or a delay might have negative consequences such as someone else getting stuck in their work progress. The other type is high priority tasks. You should do first that which is most important. For most PhD students, that will mean making a start on the literature review rather than starting to clean the windows.

The second recommendation related to task prioritisation also has to do with task importance. It is based on an anecdote involving John D. Rockefeller, who once was asked how he managed to be so productive and successful. Rockefeller allegedly explained that he categorised tasks into three categories: the 'A' tasks which were the most important and needed to be done promptly, the 'B' tasks which were important but not as critical as the A tasks, and the 'C' tasks which could be addressed if additional time could be found. Rockefeller recommended *always* starting with the A tasks. This anecdote underscores the importance of always prioritising what really matters and of avoiding spreading yourself too thinly by trying to do everything.

I find this anecdote incredibly helpful. Only last week I had an intense discussion with one of my PhD students: she wanted to run another study for her PhD which she finds interesting and easy. However, she already has enough empirical material for her PhD, and what she really needed to do was tackle her literature review write-up, which she finds hard and unpleasant, and which she was trying to put off. The literature review is the 'A' task, I said to her, with reference to Rockefeller. Just like swallowing a bitter medicine that is unpalatable but will ultimately make you better, her tackling her unpleasant 'A' task is what will ensure her ultimate PhD success.

The emphasis on identifying the most important task, planning ahead on how to tackle it (e.g., by breaking it into smaller chunks), and then simply getting started on it in a bloody-minded way is a piece of advice that features heavily in other productivity advice too. For example, in the book *Eat That Frog!*, the suggestion is also to engage in clear goal setting, and then starting immediately on the most challenging task, excluding from focus other things further down the list. This is more easily said than done, but in many ways, there is only one way to complete your PhD: just start on it. And then chip away at it, once small goal at a time.

## It doesn't have to be perfect, but it has to be you

Because a PhD seems like such an incredible and almost unattainable goal to many PhD students at the start of their journey, there can be a tendency to assume that every chapter has to be perfect. This mindset can be a great hindrance for your ability to produce anything at all: those who think their work has to be perfect often don't even start, because they are paralysed by the knowledge that whatever they produce will inevitably be flawed. Those who think their work has to be perfect before they even share a first draft with their supervisor will never share that first draft. The best thing you can do for ensuring that you make progress is to promise yourself to get something on paper every week. Once you have something black on white, this gives you a base to work from. The base won't be perfect, the final product won't be perfect, but it will be a starting point; it will be something. And something is better than nothing.

A PhD thesis is usually written within a well-defined scholarly 'straight-jacket': established formats, disciplinary conventions, and customs of reporting that ensure clarity, rigour, and comparability. These conventions are indispensable for communicating knowledge within a scientific community. Yet they should not deter you from expressing your own point of view and intellectual personality. A doctorate is not meant to be a purely mechanical exercise in following rules; it is a demonstration that you can think independently, critically, and creatively within them. Bringing your own perspective into a PhD does not mean abandoning objectivity or methodological discipline. Rather, it means taking responsibility for the choices that inevitably shape research: which questions are asked, which methods are prioritised, and how results are interpreted. How, then, can you bring your own personality into the process when science is supposed to be objective? Debates about scientific objectivity – from Kuhn's paradigms to more recent discussions of standpoint epistemology – show that science is never conducted from a neutral viewpoint. Scientific knowledge is produced by situated researchers, and objectivity arises not from the denial of perspective, but from reflexivity, transparency, and critical engagement with one's assumptions. For many students, allowing their own voice to emerge requires a degree of self-confidence that may be lacking at the start of the PhD journey. Early stages are often dominated by learning existing about the existing literature, mastering methods, and conforming to expectations. Over time, students should acquire the confidence to defend their interpretative decisions, frame problems in their own way, and articulate why their contribution matters beyond technical correctness. This might entail challenging the supervisor's directives and guidance in a way that you might not dare to do at the start of your journey! The tension between a unique perspective and conventional scientific reporting is something you will hopefully learn to navigate as you progress through your PhD. The aim is not to escape the straight-jacket, but to inhabit it thoughtfully – respecting disciplinary norms while allowing your intellectual identity, curiosity, and critical stance to shine through. After all, the PhD is your own; it is a process that will allow you to develop your unique scholarly voice. This is maybe more important now than ever before, with the advent of AI leading to a proliferation of opportunities for plagiarism and murky source accreditation. A PhD is not a piece of paper to be obtained for professional advancement through methods of cheating – it is an enriching learning experience and a journey of intellectual as well as self-discovery. Have confidence, and don't take any shortcuts.

## Collaborating well

Academia requires a high degree of self-directed and solitary work, compared to most other work settings. Maybe unsurprisingly, many academics tend to be introverts and well suited to this type of work. However, no person is an island, not even in academia. Most PhD students do need to work with others and manage upwards (their supervisors), laterally (other lab or research group members or peers), and downwards (e.g., undergraduate students, if they have teaching obligations). Therefore, it pays off to reflect on the factors that make for fruitful working relationships and smooth collaborations. Collaborating well as a PhD student is an essential skill and, like any art, it requires intention, communication, and adaptability. Effective collaboration begins with clear expectations: early conversations with supervisors and lab members about roles, timelines, authorship, and goals can prevent misunderstandings later (more on this in Chapter 4). Regular, respectful communication is equally important – updating collaborators on progress, asking for feedback, and responding thoughtfully to suggestions help build trust and momentum. Listening is as critical as contributing; being open to critique and valuing diverse perspectives strengthen both the research and the working relationship. This is – of course – more easily said that done, and whole books have been written on how to best give and receive constructive criticism. A certain level of emotional maturity will no doubt come in handy in preventing knee-jerk reactions to emotionally challenging feedback. Conflict is sometimes unavoidable, but approaching disagreements with curiosity rather than defensiveness can turn tension into productive dialogue.

Successful collaboration also requires self-advocacy. As a PhD student you should feel empowered to voice concerns, ask questions, and clarify boundaries when workloads or expectations become unclear, even when talking to seniors. Reliability also matters: meeting deadlines, following through on commitments, and being prepared for meetings signal professionalism and respect for others' time. Finally, recognising that every collaborator has different priorities, pressures, and communication styles allows you to navigate relationships with empathy. When approached thoughtfully, collaboration not only advances research but also fosters a supportive and intellectually rich academic environment that can help you thrive.

## Reward yourself

Many academics, especially the successful research types leading big labs, are incredibly driven. They always have their eye on the next achievement, the next keynote invitation, award, or high-impact publication, rather than on the achievements they have accrued to date. Many of my most successful peers have a 'glass half full' rather than a 'glass half empty' mindset – the focus tends to be on what is still missing, rather than on what is already there. This does seem to be an outlook that spurs people on to achieve more, to aim higher, to put even more effort in. But it is not an outlook that is necessarily good for well-being (see Chapter 5). In order to feel happy with ourselves and our achievements, we need the occasional proverbial pat on the shoulder both from others who matter to us and from ourselves.

What I am trying to teach my PhD students is to develop a dual focus, both on the portion of the glass that is half empty AND on the portion that is half full. It is possible to be conscious of what needs to be achieved next, but also to be conscious and proud of what has already been done. It is important to celebrate milestones, be this your upgrade, you finishing that chapter, your first publication. Doing a PhD is hard work, and the least we can do is try to give ourselves proper credit where credit is due.

I myself am one of those academics who tend to focus on goals not yet achieved, rather than on goals I have achieved. For years, I structured my working life around long to-do lists. Ticking things off my list did (and does) give me tremendous satisfaction, but the fundamental problem with any to-do list is: it is never empty. As soon as you tick one goal off, that goal gets forgotten and a new one gets added. Like Sisyphus, you end up perpetually rolling your big boulder up the hill without a chance to ever truly reach the top. This can lead to burnout. The single most effective thing I have done to achieve a healthier mindset myself is to supplement my 'to-do' list with a 'done' list. When I complete a task, I move it across to my 'other' list. Every now and again, I look at my 'done' list, and this goes a long way in helping me refocus on not only what lies ahead, but also what has been accomplished. I can recommend it unreservedly; it can have a transformative effect in terms of looking at the whole glass, not only the empty part of it. It can make you much more aware of all the things you have already achieved in the last week, month, or year, and you will feel much prouder and happier with your achievements.

A colleague who I once spoke to about this has a different tip for injecting positivity into the academic work process: she swears by celebrating small victories. There are many things that do not have the desired outcome in academia: papers get rejected, grant proposals get rejected, conference applications get rejected, and so on. This makes it all the more important to acknowledge, highlight, and celebrate when things go right. My colleague makes sure she marks every small success of her PhD students, even if it is very small. Yes, the batch of marking was only the first one of three, but it is done! Yes, the paper was published only in a minor journal, but it's been published! Her solution is different to my 'done' list, but the objective is the same: to refocus the gaze from the negative to the positive.

## Top tips

1 Work out which work routine works best for you and stick to it. Make sure your work routine includes proper, guilt-free time off.
2 Make sure you know what work is expected of you and how much time you have to complete it in total. Once you know these parameters, you can break down the work into smaller steps and deliverables and produce a timetable with sub-goals and milestones to fit the work into the available time.

3 Make sure you monitor your progress towards your goals regularly with your supervisor. You will need regular input from your supervisor: make sure you establish a pattern of regular meetings with them.
4 Remember that your work will never be perfect and that that's OK, and reward yourself regularly for work you have completed and achievements you have had on your journey.

# 4 Choosing and managing your supervisor

## The importance of the right supervisor

As anyone who has ever had a difficult boss will know, a line manager who is unreasonable, unclear, overly demanding, or unfair can make your life exceedingly difficult. In contrast, a mentor who is encouraging and who really cares about you and your progress can provide invaluable support. Your PhD supervisor is your line manager, guide, teacher, and mentor all rolled into one. The relationship between supervisor and PhD student is one of the closest working relationships that exist. In most other jobs, you do not work extremely closely on just one thing with just one person, for several years straight. Moreover, in most other jobs your line manager will typically expect that you already know how to do the work and will not need to have contact with you in order to teach you how to do the job as you go along. The intensity of the PhD supervision set-up means that committing to the wrong person can have disastrous consequences. I have witnessed several occasions where students dropped out from the PhD programme because of poor supervision. A whole lot of time, energy, and money went to waste for reasons the student was not to blame for. Finding the right person who will support you in the best way is of pivotal importance. But how to go about finding this person? In Chapter 2, we already discussed some of the principles for choosing your supervisor, but because of its importance this topic bears looking at in further detail.

Research your potential supervisor carefully. This involves googling your supervisor as well as 'interviewing' them. Any supervisor worth their salt will be happy to have a conversation with you before you mutually decide to commit to each other. Use this as an opportunity to ask them about the completion rate of their PhD students, supervision track record, and supervision philosophy. Don't be shy and ask if they have any current or former PhD students you could talk to in order to ask about their experience. Would current students recommend this person? Would they choose them

DOI: 10.4324/9781003630074-4

again if they could go back? If you have links with other people working in your chosen academic field, ask them about the supervisor too. Do they have a reputation for caring about their students or not?

I have, on a number of occasions, had people move halfway around the word to come to work with me. Some of those students acted on personal recommendations, for example when a teacher in their country knew and recommended me. But some other students went into our collaboration pretty blindly: I had vetted them, but they landed upon me more or less by chance. Let's pause and let this sink in for a moment. Moving to another city, or maybe even another country or continent, potentially speaking a different language, to work intensely for at least three years with a person you have never met face-to-face before and who you know very little about but who you will be very dependent upon bears huge risks. Given how badly things can go wrong, do try and do your homework and find out as much about your supervisor as you can in advance, before committing to them.

Once again, I must stress that what I am describing here is primarily focused on the UK system. In the USA, there is usually more classroom-based work assessed by coursework or exam before the research project itself starts, so there is less focus on doing narrow but deep research with your supervisor. Moreover, there is usually a panel of 3–5 advisors, which can make the working relationship with the primary supervisor less intense. So, in some countries there are factors that 'dilute down' the intensity of the student-supervisor relationship, which can be beneficial if things are not going smoothly. Regardless, the principle still holds: if you embark on a long-term working relationship with anyone, it is a good idea to vet them first.

There is good evidence that a positive mentoring relationship with your supervisor is one of the most important factors contributing to PhD satisfaction and happiness during your studies. Sure, being financially reasonably comfortable and having a manageable workload matter, but having a positive connection to your supervisor is absolutely crucial for student well-being. This is borne out by survey results that chart the effects of different factors on student satisfaction. Two components matter: the first one is about face time with your supervisor – many students feel that they do not see their supervisors enough and, relatedly, that they do not receive sufficient or sufficiently prompt feedback on their work. The second component is the temperature of the relationship – does the supervisor act in a supportive, attentive, empathetic manner, or are they distracted by other priorities? Do they care? Positive supervision can boost morale and performance. Interestingly, these results mirror results found with regard to therapy effectiveness. A large-scale review of which theoretical approach to psychological therapy was linked to improvements in patients found that actually, what mattered most was not the theoretical approach, but the quality of the relationship between client and therapist. Of course, the relationship between a student and their supervisor is very different to the relationship between a client and their therapist, and the intention is not to claim that the dynamics are the same. What is the same though, and what holds across both dyadic dynamics, is the fact that the human dimension matters hugely. If you manage to find a supervisor who isn't only an expert in the field that interests you but also a skilled mentor, you will be excellently set up to succeed in your PhD journey.

## Would you be happiest in the large lab of a research star or in a smaller group?

Academia is a very unequal place. Some researchers have huge research groups, also referred to in the sciences as 'research labs,' with many PostDocs, PhD students, and impressive levels of funding. Other academics operate pretty much as one-man or one-woman bands; they work by themselves and might not even have any current postgraduate students. There are also differences between disciplines: in the humanities academics tend to be sole operators, and in the natural sciences they tend to operate in large labs (in the social sciences, both models exist). The bottom line is that there is variation in terms of how different potential supervisors might be set up and resourced. In which kind of place would you be happiest?

In some ways, the question is like the question whether it is better to grow up in a large family or as a single child. There are advantages and disadvantages to both: if your supervisor does not have a large group, they should be able to give you more individual attention because they have more time just for you. But if you are in a large lab, you will also benefit from the advice and support from your postgraduate peers. Developmental psychologists know that learning during childhood does not only come from interactions with parents and teachers, but crucially also from interactions with friends and siblings. The learning that can come from frequent interactions with other lab members and mutual peer support should not be underestimated.

The sibling analogy to large labs goes further than just an opportunity for learning from peers. Just like there is often intense rivalry among siblings, this can also be an issue in large labs. On several occasions I have witnessed frustrations and conflicts between students being supervised by the same person because of a perception that there was a 'favourite' who received more attention than the others. Of course, if you choose a supervisor for whom you will be an 'only child,' this is an issue you won't have to worry about!

A question worth asking when considering joining the lab of a 'big name' person is how they got to be so big in the first place. Some senior people seem to publish more papers in prestigious outlets as lead authors than seems humanly possible. Do they achieve this by being a genius or by exploiting junior team members and taking the credit for work that was in reality done by others? The power structures in academia can make it exceedingly difficult for junior people to fight back if a senior person chooses to operate in unfair and exploitative ways. This can be a danger when working with highly successful academics who lead large labs. To mitigate against this, asking other lab members questions about the lead researcher before committing to them, as outlined above, can be very insightful.

On the other hand, being a member of a big lab headed by a 'star' can have advantages. Big names can open doors. Having the stamp of approval (e.g., a positive reference) by a leader in the field carries considerable cachet in the eyes of many. Moreover, as a student you are dependent on your supervisor being able to guide your decision making: you need your supervisor to be able to advise which conferences are worth attending, which journals are worth to targeting as publication outlets for your outputs, how to obtain funding for future study, and how to prepare yourself best for industry if you wish to leave academia after completion of your PhD. 'Big names' can safely be assumed to be 'in the know' and to know their way around the field sufficiently to have sound judgement in these matters.

Overall, there are advantages and drawbacks to both large and small teams. In smaller teams, there is potential for more individualised attention, less danger of conflict and rivalry between peers, and possibly less danger that a big star supervisor shores up their reputation by passing the work of lab members off as their own. In big labs of research stars, there are potentially great benefits to be gained through peer learning and peer support, the supervisor is likely to have necessary networks and knowledge to be very well placed to advise you on how to 'play the game' and advance your career, and their reference and recommendation will count for a lot. There is probably no 'one size fits all' solution when it comes to choosing a big or small lab. Your own preferences and personality might also inform in which context you would be happier. Both large and small family set-ups can constitute healthy environments for children to grow up in, and the same is true for 'academic families.' But it does payoff to be aware of the potential pitfalls of both contexts and to potentially troubleshoot and address concerns you might have as you journey down your path. You might wonder though: if there is a need to troubleshoot, how do you go about that? Who to complain to when things go wrong?

## Advantages and disadvantages of solo supervision versus team supervision

In the UK, traditionally PhD students used to have just one academic supervisor. In some other countries such as the USA, team supervision is the common model. Increasingly, team supervision is now also becoming more common in the UK. Crucially, if the student has concerns about the working relationship with one supervisor, in a team setting they have the option of turning to other mentors for support.

The move in the UK towards team supervision is maybe partially driven by an increased popularity of interdisciplinarity in the research funding landscape. Two supervisors might have complementary expertise, especially if they come from different disciplinary backgrounds, so the thinking. The move towards team supervision might also partially be the result of a desire to take the pressure out of the intensity of a one-to-one set-up between just one student and just one supervisor. A larger supervisory team can provide more expertise and resources for one student to benefit from and can afford the student with a richer experience, and maybe also reduce the supervisory burden on each individual supervisor.

The model of dual supervision is, however, also not without risk: I have seen cases where intense conflict erupted between supervisors about methodological approaches or other choices relevant to the work. If two big egos clash, the PhD student might be left stuck in the middle and unsure whose advice to listen to and to whom to stay loyal. Just as children can suffer during acrimonious divorce, so PhD students can suffer when conflict erupts between supervisors.

In cases where there is only one academic supervisor, students are sometimes assigned an 'advisor,' whose sole remit is to be a point of contact if there are any welfare concerns the student might have. The advisor has a pastoral role and can function as mediator and support network if problems arise between the student and supervisor. In cases of relationship breakdown or trouble with the supervisor, an advisor can provide a vital safety net. Like a mediator in a legal dispute, the advisor must be skilled in conflict management and must approach disagreements with sufficient empathy and neutrality. Elevated levels of interpersonal competence are needed to navigate situations where there is strong tension between the supervisor and student. Such tensions can arise for many reasons: unvoiced or unmet expectations, or unreasonable behaviour on one or both sides. I have witnessed cases of complete relationship breakdown between supervisor and student where an inexperienced advisor made the situation worse with their naïve meddling. However, in many cases a model where the student can draw on one key contact for academic advice and on another key contact for pastoral advice and support in case there are issues with the supervisor works very well. In any case, getting clarity about the supervision model at your chosen institution before committing to do your PhD there can be immensely helpful.

## Your relationship with your supervisor: parallels with family relations

A bunch of psychological studies demonstrate that people do not come to work as 'tabula rasas'; they bring their personalities, hang-ups, and expectations to work in ways that fundamentally affect relationships at work. If we encounter a new person who reminds us of a significant other from our previous life, then we might often be tempted to subconsciously project our previous experiences and expectations onto the new person. For example, if you grew up with an overbearing 'smart-ass' brother and one of your peers looks a bit like your brother, you might be on the lookout for this person to act condescendingly towards you, and you might react with particular sensitiveness when you sense such intent in this colleague. If you grew up with a dad prone to unpredictable aggression, you might project this onto your PhD supervisor and be anxious about upsetting them because you fear angry outbursts. Given the strong dependency between PhD student and PhD supervisor, it is hardly surprising that this relationship often provides a fruitful ground for projections. These projections are often automatic, subconscious, and therefore hard to stop or change. Our best chance to interact with others at work maturely and consciously is to try and be aware of biases we bring to the situation, as much as we can. Whenever interactions with others at work prove challenging, when someone appears incompetent, disorganised, unreasonable, domineering, it is worth asking: how much of my reaction is to do with their objective behaviour? What do I bring to the situation? How much is this to do with them, and how much is the issue to do with me?

Above, I talked about how there are parallels between the dynamics found in large or small labs to the dynamics found in large or small families. There can also be parallels between the student-supervisor relationship and that between child and parent. In many ways, a PhD is a rite of passage, a 'coming of age' process, the path from naivety and dependence to intellectual maturity and independence. Small children who are dependent on their parents glorify them in early childhood. The parent seems strong, infallible, and omnipotent. This then changes in puberty as the child establishes greater independence. Suddenly the parent is questioned, criticised, or even rejected. I have seen a similar process play out many times as students move thorough their PhD. At the start, the intense and often slightly claustrophobic student-teacher relationship is such that the student is totally naïve and is dependent on the supervisor to guide the way. The supervisor appears saintly or even Godly in their knowledge and wisdom. Then, as students begin to learn, question, and form their own opinions, they begin to see the supervisor's limitations. Some frustrations with the supervisor's limitations might be realistically related to the supervisor's shortcomings. However, the supervisor might also be used as a scapegoat. Completing a PhD is often intensely frustrating. Many things can go wrong and be experienced as difficult, and the supervisor can be a welcome scapegoat. 'She should have told me about this earlier,' 'he didn't provide me with sufficient guidance,' and 'his understanding of the problem is really superficial' are things I have heard PhD students say about their supervisors during the throes of their PhD work. In the eyes of the student, the supervisor's image can oscillate between that of a saint and that of a devil. Doing a PhD can be like going through puberty in terms of how students see the supervisor: from glorification to rejection to final appreciation of both the supervisor's strengths and limitations. Take heart in knowing this: if you are in the middle of your PhD and your supervisor is driving you up the wall, you are not alone. In some ways, it is part of the process.

## Power imbalances: beware of exploitation

Of course, there are instances where frustrations with and concerns about the supervisor are not merely part of a 'normal developmental trajectory' of going through a PhD, but where they are rooted in deeply problematic behaviour on the part of the supervisor. Unfortunately, sexual harassment and exploitation are issues in many workplaces, and maybe especially so in academia. Many of the vital ingredients that can encourage malpractice are present in universities. The higher up you go through the ranks in academia, the more men outnumber women. So, a frequent constellation is that of a senior, older male supervisor with considerable influence and power over junior – and often young and attractive – female students. Unwanted sexual advances usually, but not always, involve male supervisors and junior female students. On top of that, as outlined in Chapter 3, many people in academia are deeply invested in their work. Work is not seen as 'work,' but many academics see it as their purpose in life, their mission, their raison d'être. By extension, colleagues might feel that they are not just work colleagues but intellectual 'soul mates' who share the same deep passions. Work does not get much more personal than that. Moreover, passionate intellectual debate is conducted not only 9 to 5 in the office, but often also at conferences in pleasant locations. Colleagues who seemed pleasant enough in the office are cast in a new light and might become considerably more enticing when sharing deep conversation over red wine sitting on a medieval square in southern Spain or sitting on an idyllic beach in California. As the criminologist knows, for a deed to occur what is needed are motive, means, and opportunity. Senior (male) supervisors tend to have all three: exposure to young students that are sexually enticing (motive), power over those students (means), and access to those students through work practices that encourage encounters outside the office, for example during academic conferences (opportunity). No wonder, then, that sexual advances frequently result. I am personally aware of a mind-boggling number of cases where work relations between supervisor and student that were appropriately sober initially later turned into something else.

For some of those cases, the attraction is entirely one-sided. I know of female students who have felt hugely pressured and harassed by their supervisors, very much against their own preference and much to their distress. The senior party, in this scenario, of course also make themselves vulnerable to considerable risk: it is pleasing to see that sexual misconduct at universities is increasingly being addressed, with sexual predators now being brought to justice where for many decades they got away with unacceptable behaviour. In my own field, I have seen some senior male colleagues recently lose their positions over their treatment of junior female students, and an increasing awareness of the unacceptability of sexual exploitation in higher education and other sectors is long overdue and most welcome.

Having said this, it is also true that attraction between supervisor and student is sometimes mutual and reciprocated. To a new, young PhD student who is still trying to work out the lay of the land in their new work environment or even in life in general, the supervisor can appear as admirably distinguished, powerful, and attractive. It is a well-known fact that hostages sometimes fall for their hostage-takers; this phenomenon has been called Stockholm syndrome. There is something about being dependent on a powerful other that can elicit a psychological response of attraction. This is psychological dynamic that can be very much present between student and supervisor. What, then, to make of those situations where both supervisor *and* student want to see their relationship progress beyond a purely professional one?

Many universities have explicit policies against romantic involvement between teachers and students, in recognition of the fact that romantic involvement that is based on a strong power imbalance violates key ethical and safeguarding rules. Some, but not all, universities have rules against romantic involvements between colleagues developing. The position of a PhD student within most UK departments falls between the two chairs of student and colleague: neither true 'student' nor true 'colleague,' PhD students are often seen as something in between. I believe it is difficult to say that romantic involvement between student and supervisor is wrong in any case. I do know of several couples that were formed during PhD supervision, some of them turning into decade-long happy relationships. However, any PhD student who entertains entering such a set-up would be well advised to do so with open eyes: yours is a relationship with a very specific dynamic, and a dynamic that disadvantages you. As the less powerful party, you are vulnerable to exploitation. Be aware of this and mindful of safeguarding your interests.

## Getting your supervisor to give you what you need

Not everyone needs the same type of support. I have been constantly amazed just by how different the needs of my different PhD students have been. Some of my students are excellent at having many creative ideas but are unable to decide what to focus on or to create a structure to translate their creativity into something concrete. Others are extremely good at programme management but need support in understanding how their work can and must go beyond what has already been published in the literature. Some of my students need me to create some light pressure and deadlines in order to galvanise them into action, and others decidedly do not need such pressure as this would be overwhelming and anxiety producing for them. Some students write beautiful narratives but only have an incomplete understanding of methodology; others have a firm grasp of methods but need a lot of help correcting their prose. Some students need more guidance; others need more freedom to explore by themselves. What is it that you need from your supervisor? It is important to identify this, because awareness of your unique strengths and development needs will enable you to better guide your supervisor towards supporting you in a way that works for you.

The list of students' potential strengths and weaknesses is potentially very long (true for supervisors too!). If you strive for clarity what your own strengths and limitations are, pondering your own profile will help you understand what support you would benefit from the most and what you should be asking for. Take some time to make a list of what you think your strong points and your development needs are and write those down. It can also be helpful to ask your friends and those who have worked with you in the past for their insights. Have a frank conversation with your supervisor about this, so that your supervisor has the information needed to know how best to support you. We all have a tendency to assume that the world looks to everyone like it looks from our perspective. There can be an inclination to assume that if something is obvious to you, it must surely also be evident and visible to your supervisor. However, often it will not be. Therefore, there is no such thing as 'overcommunicating' when it comes to letting your supervisor know how they can best support you. Telling your supervisor clearly what you need is your best bet to ensuring that you will get it. A good supervisor will always make time to listen to your concerns.

To help you start thinking about this more, here are some key competencies that are needed, according to my experience, to successfully complete a PhD. No student has the 'full package', and we all have development needs, but these are some of the key skills you can either capitalise on or work on, besides research, analytical, and technical skills: creativity, an ability to structure ideas, time- and project management skills, communication skills, ability to resist perfectionism, and self-confidence.

A PhD is supposed to create something new and develop new understanding and insights that did not previously exist. To achieve that, you must be able to look at the literature and understand where the gaps are, and to think outside the box. Some students are naturally better at this than others, but it is a skill that can also be improved with practice. PhD students must also be excellent at structuring material and ideas. After having read 100 peer-reviewed articles by experts on a certain topic, what are the key themes? What are the emerging insights? How can the material be structured into a logical sequence? As a PhD student you will also need excellent time- and project management skills. I have already reflected in Chapter 3 on what this entails in more detail, and on the fact that many PhD students struggle with this initially. However, this too is a skill that can be improved with practice for those to whom it doesn't come naturally. PhD students clearly need excellent communication skills, both orally (e.g., when presenting their work at academic conferences, or when talking to their supervisor about the challenges they are facing in their work) and in written form when producing the PhD thesis. What is your key message you want to bring across? How do you best present this message with maximum clarity? Another key skill PhD students must possess is the ability to strive for excellence, not perfection (see also the reflections on perfectionism in Chapter 3). Yes, your work needs to be of a high standard, and submitting work littered with errors and typos will not be sufficient. At the same time, your work will never be perfect. It is a fine art to decide when you have reached the point of 'good enough,' and it is something some PhD students must painfully learn before they master this judgement sure-footedly. The last aspect on my suggested list above was 'self-confidence.' This might be somewhat surprising because confidence is not so much, like the other aspects that were listed, a 'skill,' but it is more of a 'personal attribute.' Yet, it is also essential for succeeding in your PhD and your life post-PhD. You need to have a certain level of confidence in your judgement to make a decision about which line of enquiry to pursue and which one to put on the back burner. You need to acquire confidence in your judgement about what the best methods are to investigate your chosen topic. Last but not least, you need confidence in your ideas and yourself in order to successfully 'sell' them to others and persuade others of the validity and value of what you are adding to the world. It is not for nothing that we say 'fake it until you make it': portraying self-confidence outwardly will make it easier for others to start having confidence in you. A good supervisor will always empower you to feel more and more confident, and if you feel that interactions with your supervisor have the opposite effects, alarm bells should be ringing.

This list of skills needed to complete a PhD is, of course, not exhaustive, and the attributes mentioned here can be added to those already discussed in Chapter 1. The crucial point is that it pays off to reflect on what is needed, what you do well, and where you need additional support. To gain clarity, speak to your supervisor about it to enable them to best support you. Of course, it is not only students who have different strengths and development needs, but supervisors also are not equally good at everything. Some supervisors are more empathic, more diligent, faster at providing feedback, more invested in their students' success. Some are also more resourceful than others: one supervisor might have many funds in their lab and might be able to support you financially when you need a six-month extension; others are not in that position. Comparisons of how different supervisors within one department do or do not support their respective students are the topic of many discussions among PhD peers. Such discussions are also useful for calibrating what a reasonable level of support might look like. Before you complain about not receiving enough guidance or not receiving feedback quickly enough, it is helpful to understand the norms and expectations. This can often be gleamed by official documentation setting out supervisory expectations by the university, but it can also be gleamed by hearing what support peers are receiving. For example, if you are unsure whether waiting for feedback for two weeks is reasonable or not, knowing that one of your friends always gets feedback within two days and the other friend never gets feedback more quickly than two months later are helpful benchmarks for comparison.

I have discussed elsewhere the importance of regular meetings with your supervisor, but it is no use seeing your PhD supervisor frequently if those meetings are not productive. Often, PhD students leave their supervisor's office with a feeling that they have absolutely no idea what their supervisor wants them to do next. This is to be avoided. If your supervisor is not good at setting clear objectives and agreeing clear targets, make it your job to clarify those. At the end of each meeting, ask the supervisor to agree a summary of actions that you (or they!) will follow up, and agree a timeline for those. This is also a useful strategy to help with another frequent issue: supervisors are often busy people with lots on their mind. Some of them are really quite scatty too, with their head in the clouds.

This means that often when you go to meet them, they might have entirely forgotten everything you discussed last time and might first require a high-level summary. I used to find this quite frustrating when working with a supervisor like that during my undergraduate project. I could not quite comprehend how anyone could possibly have such short-term memory, and I will confess finding it more than a little irritating. Now, I am acutely conscious of inflicting the same on my own students, who often look at me in bewilderment when I require reminding of something that is entirely obvious to them. Be forgiving of your supervisor's limitations and quirks, after all they are only human. At the same time, it is their job to give you attention, feedback, and help, and if this is not sufficiently forthcoming don't be shy to complain about that.

One factor that is in your influence, and that might just affect the support you get from your supervisor, is what you ask of them. In an ideal world, your supervisor is a skilled and experienced mentor who knows exactly what you need and supplies it without you having to ask for it. However, this is a rare scenario. As a PhD student, the PhD is essentially your work; it is your name that will be written on the front cover. So, don't be afraid to get in the driver's seat. If your supervisor is too scatty or too busy to schedule regular meetings, ask them concretely for what you need. Asking for a 1-hour meeting every week, if that is what you would like to support your progress, is a reasonable request. Your supervisor might not agree, but at least if they know exactly what level of support you are looking for, they can consider it, and you can have a conversation around it. You can ask for the meetings to be pre-scheduled rather than ad hoc, to ensure they do not fall off the radar and to maintain a certain regularity in order to keep up the pace and structure your work towards clear intermediate deadlines and deliverables. If your supervisor cancels a meeting, don't be afraid to follow up and ask for it to be rescheduled.

One outcome of every meeting should aim for is clarity around what you are expected to do next, and by when. If at the end of the meeting the actions (both for you and the supervisor!) are vague and unclear, do not feel afraid to ask for greater clarity. Clear communication is not necessarily the forte of all academics, and you are completely within your rights to expect that next steps should be clearly defined and agreed. If your supervisor is not a person who is naturally good at translating intellectual discussion into actionable deliverables, help them by asking for greater clarity. That way, you can negotiate the next steps that both of you need to take. Clarity should also exist not only in relation to the timetable of deliverables, but also in relation to the content. You will be unable to produce high-quality work unless you know what 'good looks like' and what the criteria are that your work will be measured by. These might be blatantly obvious to you, or rather obscure, especially if you are new to your country of study, unfamiliar with the education system in that country, or don't have an extensive social network that can initiate you (e.g., if you are a first gen or otherwise minoritised student). If you are not clear on the criteria and expectations, do not shy away from asking your supervisor for clarification – it is their job to guide you in this regard. There is no such thing as a stupid question.

Another 'resource' you will need from your supervisor is timely feedback. They will need to provide periodic feedback on your written work and ultimately the whole thesis before submission. It can be uncomfortable to send off a chapter for feedback, and not have any idea how long it might take the supervisor to respond. So, ask for clarification. It is entirely reasonable to ask whether the supervisor is able to turn the work around within a certain timeframe or by a certain date. If they cannot work as quickly as you would like them to, at least if you request clear information on when the feedback can be expected, you are in a better position to structure your own next work steps whilst you wait for the feedback. It might also help the supervisor to know in advance when to expect your work, so that they can consider the impact on their own schedule and block out time. If you communicate clearly and in advance, for example, that you will get a chapter to them by the end of the month, and ask if you can expect to receive feedback by two weeks later, you and your supervisor are both in an excellent position to plan ahead and avoid lengthy waiting periods of the clustering of work during a period where your supervisor has lots of other demands on their time.

One humorous piece of advice I have come across is to treat your PhD supervisor as a goldfish. Assume that they forget everything about you and your project as soon as you step out of the door. Be prepared to remind them of key facts that are blatantly obvious to you at the start of the next meeting. Be prepared to do this every single time you meet them. I have certainly been at the receiving end of this as a student (interestingly, not in relation to my own PhD supervisor, but when working with other academics). Many professors do seem to live up to the stereotype of the scatty academic who require reminding of even the most basic of facts. The fact that humorous advice like the 'goldfish' advice exists suggests that this is indeed not an isolated phenomenon. Whilst this might be intensely annoying to some students, there is a reason why this dynamic arises: the student typically thinks only about their project and little else. They engage with it in a very deep and intense way. The supervisor, on the other hand, is likely to be in a position where they need to juggle a myriad of other obligations and demands; their mind needs to flit between different projects and priorities, making it hard to be equally enmeshed in the student's work. Try to be kind to your supervisor when you have to explain the obvious repeatedly – they are not disengaged; they are likely doing their very best.

You cannot control what your supervisor is able and willing to offer you, but you can guide them in the right direction and create optimal conditions by asking clearly for what you need: (a) make sure they know what you need, both in terms of your individual personality and in terms of meeting frequency and input, and clearly communicate this to your supervisor; (b) ensure that you leave meetings with them with clarity on all sides about what the next steps are and who will do what by when, and if you do not have this clarity, then ask; and (c) know where to get support when things go wrong with your supervisor and there is a need for troubleshooting. Is there support you can get from an advisor, a second supervisor or someone else in the doctoral school? Make sure you know where you can turn to.

## Top tips

1 Make sure you vet the PhD supervisor you are committing to! Try to ascertain, as much as possible, that they are a 'good cookie' before signing on the dotted line.
2 Consider the advantages and drawbacks of being in a big lab or working with an individual. Where would you personally be happiest? Similarly, ask questions about solo versus team supervision and whether you would have an advisor responsible for your pastoral care. Make sure you only commit to a place where you feel you would be well looked after.
3 Remember: if your view of your supervisor changes as you move through the PhD process, this is only normal! Your supervisor is probably not quite as wonderful as you think at the start, and probably not quite as horrible as you might think when you are in the thick of it. Importantly, if you are the victim of sexual harassment or unwelcome sexual advances, speak up and seek help. No one should be able to get away with exploiting their dependents.
4 To get the best out of your supervisor, be clear on your strengths and development needs, and clearly communicate to your supervisor how they can best support you. Make sure you know where to turn to when things go wrong.

# 5 Thriving during your PhD

## Managing your well-being

Doing a PhD can be immensely rewarding, but it can also be challenging. We have touched upon some of those challenges in previous chapters. It is useful to think a bit more deeply about the obstacles you might encounter during your PhD and how to overcome them. This is important because mental health problems among today's students seem to have reached unprecedented levels. Many studies suggest that university students these days struggle more than they used to. Some commentators argue that this is simply because the present generation is more willing to report on their struggles than previous generations, who were more likely to suffer in silence. Others suggest that the greater prevalence of reported mental health struggles is indicative of more suffering, rather than just more openness in reporting the suffering. Increased competitiveness of the job market and less job security have been cited to contribute to increased levels of anxiety and fatalism among graduates. Moreover, the COVID-19 pandemic has deprived some student cohorts of the opportunity to hang out with peers and establish strong levels of independence from primary caregivers during formative school years, with potential negative consequences later down the line when students then enter university. Lack in independence and lack of resilience are also factors that are cited by commentators who argue that young people today are often mollycoddled. Ever-hovering parents who cushion their children from real-world stressors might deprive those children from the opportunity to learn how to cope with setbacks. As a consequence, minor obstacles at university can unbalance students possibly to a greater degree than was the case in the past. There are a lot of diverging theories on the root causes of the mental health struggles prevalent among today's students. Irrespective of the cause, one thing is clear: it is important to be mindful how you can protect your mental health.

Insights into the mental health and well-being challenges that can be posed by a PhD come not only from comparing today's students with previous cohorts, but they also come from comparing the use of psychiatric medication in PhD students, compared to the time period before and

DOI: 10.4324/9781003630074-5

following a PhD. Some large-scale studies have found that PhD work coincides with a rise in the use of such medication and that it declines again after graduation. This pattern seems to be pretty stable across different fields, genders, and socioeconomic groups. It is indeed suggestive of the challenges posed by PhD work. It also poses questions about the prevalent structure and culture of academic work and encourages university leaders to reflect on them. To be sure, such statistics should not put anyone off embarking on a PhD if that is their dream. Averages always hide huge individual variation. It is possible to thrive and positively enjoy the PhD experience, and I know many people who have. At the same time, if you do feel yourself struggling at any point during your PhD, there can be comfort in knowing that this is not an isolated experience, but something that a significant number of peers also go through. The onus of considering how early-career researchers can best be supported to avoid psychological distress is clearly on university leaders. At the same time, there are steps you can take to look after yourself, and doing this can be very empowering. Positively addressing one's mental health requires, in the first instance, awareness of the factors that might pose challenges.

Some of the factors discussed in previous chapters which can potentially put a strain on well-being during your PhD were: being trapped in a spiral of procrastination, never being 'off,' an inability to break down the big task into bite-sized chunks, perfectionism, a reluctance to celebrate and give yourself credit for achievements, and not asking for or not receiving the right support from your PhD supervisor. What are other factors that can pose a risk to your well-being? You can boost yourself against factors that detrimentally affect your well-being by being aware of them and by putting the right protective measures into place to ensure you are supported. Being aware of potential pitfalls and having a plan how to avoid them will put you in excellent stead to emerge from your studies not only academically successful, but also happy and healthy.

## The half empty glass: avoiding burnout

One of the most important factors has already been discussed in Chapter 3, but this issue looms so large that it is worth looking at it in more detail. The trouble with academia is that the work is never 'done.' In many other jobs, people work 9–5 and know that after 5pm they can legitimately clock off and enjoy the evening without feeling they should still be at work. The feeling that you have completed your day's work and have earned yourself some downtime can be intensely refreshing and recharging. It is a feeling that many academics never experience. In academia, the ceiling of what can be accomplished is potentially infinitely high – one could always author more papers, better papers, attract more grant money, have more students, be more well known in the field, and so on. Moreover, most (if not all) academics know someone who they consider more successful than themselves and someone they feel they should try to 'catch up' with in terms of achievements and success. The feeling to need to keep pace with someone is sometimes grounded in objective reality: often a kind of 'race' can take place between two or more labs to establish a new fact, publish a new insight first, and be the first to take credit for some advance. The person who first gets their paper peer reviewed and out in the public domain will get all the credit, and the person who got there one day later is forgotten by history. All of this makes for a culture of long hours and sacrificed weekends. The constant striving for more achievement encourages attention to the things that have not yet been achieved, rather than the things that have been accomplished. You don't have to be a rocket scientist to work out that always looking for what is wanting than what is plentiful will not foster contentment and happiness. This frame of mind described here rubs off from supervisor to student and from one peer to another. PhD students are often socialised in a mindset that bears the danger of burnout. As someone embarking on your PhD journey: try to resist! Do not adopt this unhelpful outlook. There are some easy things you can do to refocus your attention to the positive, rather than the negative. Try to accept that there will always be someone who accomplishes more than you. Try not to measure yourself against other people, but against your own goals and standards that you have set yourself. Make sure to celebrate victories, no matter how small. It can be difficult, in a context where everyone always wants to achieve more, to say: 'I am enough' and 'I am doing enough.' But this realisation is absolutely essential for good mental health, so try to give yourself a break where you have deserved one.

## Loneliness

One affliction that many PhD students report suffering from is the excessive loneliness of the work. Although there are some opportunities for teamwork, and although good supervisors meet with their students regularly, at the end of the day a PhD is about one substantial piece of work authored and presented by one person. What is more, your work is likely to be so specialised that it can be hard to talk about it to lay people outside the field. There often is a lot of technical jargon or prior knowledge needed to grasp even the basic gist of it. For large parts of your PhD, it might feel like there is only you and your project on an island of solitude.

This is problematic, because it is well known that we need interactions and exchange with others, and we need the support of others to be happy and healthy. There are countless studies that support the idea that human contact is absolutely essential for human thriving. Even regular social contact of the non-intimate kind, like a brief interaction with someone in a shop, can be greatly beneficial for our well-being, and close relationships have this positive impact on our mental health even more so. Of course, many PhD students will have casual interactions in coffee shops. Many might also be in happy relationships and cultivate strong friendships. But the obsessive way in which some academics and their students engage with their work can mean that close relationships suffer. I have heard academics say that they are not able to have a romantic partner because they would not be able to fit it in with their work!

In addition to casual interactions and close intimate relationships, there is another type of relationship many people benefit from at work, and that is the feeling of being part of a team where everyone works towards a common goal. There are some scholars who argue that being part of a larger social whole is even more essential for well-being than close intimate relationships. The supportive banter at work, the chat by the coffee machine, and the daily interaction with a bunch of people who you might not consider close friends but who you nonetheless know quite well and who you enjoy spending time with are features of the workplace that are very important to many people's work satisfaction. They are also features that are much less present in the working life of many a solitary PhD student quietly squirrelling away at their project. This makes it all the more important that you as a PhD student make sure you spend enough time with your friends and close others in your life. Being with others can help you recharge your batteries. Even natural introverts need a healthy amount of regular social contact. If you feel isolated and lonely during your PhD, this is a sure sign to move away from your computer screen, pick up the phone, and spend some time with people to nourish your social bonds. There are also some things you can do to make the PhD work itself less lonely: organise writing retreats with peers at your institution or visit PhD peers working on similar issues at another university. These writing buddy schemes could be face-to-face or virtual. However you organise it, it is important to avoid becoming a hermit, and it is important to maintain social relationships and interests outside of your PhD work.

Some PhD students conduct a large chunk of their PhD work remotely, based in a location far away from the university. On occasion, the entire PhD might be supervised remotely and online. This might happen when life circumstances prevent a relocation, for example. I have successfully worked with a couple of people within this set-up, and luckily technology means that regular online check-ins are very easy nowadays, making this a more viable model. However, although it is possible to conduct a PhD in this way when there are no other options, in my view this results in a much poorer learning experience than being on campus in person. Actual physical presence at the university allows for attendance of visiting speakers' talks, methodology training, learning from and exchanging ideas with peers, and so much more. It also boosts against loneliness and isolation and allows for the supervisors to get a better sense of where a student is at. It is easier to pick up on subtle cues about how the student is copying with the work in face-to-face meetings and to intervene and offer additional support where indicated. As mentioned, even an on-campus PhD experience can feel lonely, so just imagine doing the work remotely on top of that! These aspects should be carefully considered before committing to a remote PhD and if this is an attractive model for you, you'll be well advised to build in regular visits to campus anyway, as frequently as practically feasible.

## Imposter syndrome

Much of what has been discussed so far was about how to deal with feelings of not achieving enough, not being productive enough, not working hard enough. Those anxieties are task focused, and they do – unsettling though they may be – not touch the core sense of self of the PhD student in the same way imposter syndrome does. Imposter syndrome is a generalised feeling that you as a person are not enough – not competent enough, not smart enough, not capable enough. Of course, you can change your behaviour more easily than your essential personality and character. Therefore, imposter syndrome – where you feel that you yourself are lacking rather than just the work you have recently produced is lacking – is the most gutting demon one might encounter, because it cuts to the core of your being. Have you ever wondered why you got admitted to a certain school or why you got chosen for some award, when deep down you felt like you didn't deserve it because you didn't feel competent? Have you ever worried that one day someone will find out you are really just a fraud and will kick you out of the programme or rescind whatever honour they have just bestowed upon you? If the answer to those questions is yes, then you are no stranger to imposter syndrome. Feeling this way is characterised by a lack of confidence in one's own abilities and possibly a lack of general – or at least work-related – self-esteem. Of course, sometimes people *are* promoted beyond their capabilities and are justified in fearing that they can't deliver what is expected of them. However, for those people suffering from imposter syndrome these fears are unfounded, as they are in reality very competent individuals. There has recently started to be more awareness of the syndrome, and the percentage of people who privately worry about being 'found out' as incompetent imposters is much higher than previously thought. If you suffer from severe imposter syndrome, then you might want to seek more targeted help for this, and a few words of advice on this book might not be sufficient. However, for milder cases of imposter syndrome, it might help just to know that most people have those doubts and anxieties at some point in their lives. Just knowing that you are not alone with those feelings might help normalise them and might make the worries seem less indicative of something being seriously wrong. Relatedly, it is important to realise that everyone will make mistakes during their PhD. I have never met a student who, upon completion, hadn't wished they had designed a certain study in a different way, spent more time on task A and less on task B, gone about structuring their work or their writing in a different way, or tackled a certain aspect of the work differently. A PhD is a learning process, and by definition there will be things that you know at the end that you didn't know at the beginning, and therefore by definition you will make mistakes. Making mistakes is not a problem. Everyone makes mistakes. Making mistakes is certainly not a sign that you are not cut out for or deserving of a PhD.

## Financial stress and career anxiety

It is easy to be relaxed and happy when you have plenty of funds to do what you want to do, when you don't have to worry about how to pay the rent, and when you know that you will step into a lucrative career to reap plenty of financial rewards post-PhD. Sadly, this is not the reality many PhD students find themselves in. As already mentioned, PhD studentships tend not to be generous, and the PhD life therefore does not tend to be full of luxury, at least not in the UK. Worrying about how to pay the next bill is not a recipe for happiness. What is maybe even more detrimental for mental health than financial constraints at present are worries about the future. Although a PhD can be a significant asset for job seekers, and indeed many might be tempted to pursue a PhD for that very reason, the job market overall is not as buoyant for the next generation as it once was. At present in the UK, there is a hiring decline and increased competition for graduate roles. Starting salaries have also declined once inflation is taken into account. At the same time, house prices have risen and risen, putting the prospect of owning your own home (a key aspiration for most people in the UK, unlike some other European countries) firmly out of reach for many. It is not hard to see how these factors might negatively impact on the mental health of students and other young people.

This is important to bear in mind, because mental health is clearly affected by objective external pressures, stresses, and circumstances. The factors mentioned above (burnout, loneliness, physical well-being, imposter syndrome) are more 'psychological' in nature. However, well-being is not only 'in the head,' but also tied to real-life obstacles and struggles.

Remembering this can be important to avoid the trap of victim-blaming, in this case avoiding the assumption that students who are stressed suffer at their own hand by cultivating the 'wrong' mindset. Student life is hard, and arguably harder than it used to be, and the onus is on older academics to remember this.

What practical insights might a PhD student draw from all this? To make these stressors go away, a magic wand would be needed. In the absence of this, there are a few things you can remind yourself of. First, when in a challenging situation such as a financial tight spot, it can help to remind yourself that it is temporary. The reason you have decided to put up with this is because you expect delayed rewards in the future. Second, although it is undoubtedly true that finding your first job after graduation might not be easy, it can be helpful to remind yourself that you are likely to be in a stronger position than most with a PhD certificate in hand. There is comfort in knowing that you are making the best of a challenging situation, and you can congratulate yourself for this.

## Positive steps you can take

The first things I would like to flag, and one that has been echoed by some of my own PhD students, is the importance of taking care of your body. The mind and the body are inextricably linked; there is a bidirectional relationship between mental and physical health. Feeling healthy and happy in yourself is most easily achieved in a healthy body. Our bodies were made for moving; yet PhD work is mainly sedentary. After years of sitting at a desk, your body will start adapting to those suboptimal conditions: your shoulders will get rounded during a prolonged routine of being hunched over your keyboard, your hip flexors will become shortened due to a sustained habit of sitting at a desk. This, in turn, can cause reduced hip mobility and lower back pain. Movement and physical activity cause the release of endorphins, also known as 'happiness hormones,' and those who sit at a desk all day every day miss out on that. One of the most beneficial things you can do, especially if you are likely to have a desk-based job following your PhD, is to establish a routine of interspersing physical activity throughout your day. Establish a routine of going for a walk in the morning, doing a short stretching routine after work, or regularly getting up from your desk to create some movement will yield important benefits in the long run.

Spending time in nature is also important for mental health, especially for PhD students who often face high levels of stress, long hours of work, and isolation. There is strong research evidence that nature provides a restorative environment that allows the mind to relax and recover from cognitive fatigue. Even brief exposure to green spaces – such as parks, gardens, or forests – can reduce stress, lower cortisol levels, and improve mood. Walking or sitting outdoors encourages physical activity, which in itself – as seen above – enhances mental well-being. Nature also offers a sense of perspective, helping students step back from academic pressures and reflect more clearly on challenges. Regular time outdoors can improve focus, creativity, and problem-solving skills, which are crucial for research. By integrating nature into daily routines, PhD students can cultivate resilience, reduce anxiety, and maintain a healthier work-life balance, ultimately supporting both their mental health and academic performance.

Another useful piece of advice I have heard students give each other is to celebrate small victories. Doing a PhD requires focused effort over a long period of time, which means that the positive reward (successful graduation and completion) is significantly delayed, and your day-to-day activity can feel very far removed from the end goal. This makes celebrating the intermediate steps incredibly important for keeping up morale. Related to this, it is important to set realistic goals and break down big tasks into smaller steps. Did you just finish a literature review? Did you just write a chapter, or maybe just the opening paragraph? Did you just successfully learn about a new method you are hoping to use during your PhD? Whatever it is, make sure that you reward yourself, either just by privately acknowledging those everyday victories, or maybe by celebrating with a little treat that appeals to you.

## Whose job is it anyway to look after our mental health?

One important question in relation to mental health is: whose job is it to look after students' mental health? If you are struggling with mental health during your PhD, whose job is it to remedy the situation? Traditionally (maybe up until the 1990s), mental health was primarily viewed as an individual's responsibility. With greater recognition of the fact that poor mental health is not a personal failing but can be a consequence of contextual factors, attention shifted away from the individual towards institutional and societal responsibility. In educational institutions in the USA and the UK, there is now a strong recognition of the ethical and legal duty to create supportive environments and meet mental health challenges in students as an institutional priority. Most UK universities have exponentially increased the resource they allocate to student well-being and support services.

Some commentators, for example Jonathan Haidt, have argued that this trend has gone too far. According to this view, in the race to be maximally supportive of students, anxiety and depression in students are actually encouraged by preventing students from having the opportunities needed to build resilience through exposure to manageable stressors. What has shifted is not only the mainstream view of who is responsible for mental health, but also of how much mental discomfort is acceptable or even necessary for growth.

Who, then, is responsible for your mental health as a PhD student? What would your answer be to this question? My own view would be that often if there is a question of 'is it A or B,' the answer is 'a bit of both.' The fact that poor mental health is no longer seen as an individual failing is an important improvement on the previous zeitgeist. The fact that there is more awareness of the need to create supportive environments is an important innovation. But this cannot mean that students should abdicate all responsibility for their mental health. A student who does not take ownership of and agency in relation to their mental health gives up control; they give power over to others and make themselves the plaything of external forces. This, as we know from the work of psychologist Martin Seligman on learned helplessness, is in itself a precursor to passivity and depression. As a student, you *can* influence your mental health for the better. You have agency. But it is not all up to you. You require a supportive environment. And where this does not exist, it is ok to demand change.

## Top tips

1 Avoid burnout by taking time off and celebrating your achievements. There will always be someone who is more successful, but your work is good enough and you are good enough.
2 Make sure you build a social support network around you that can counterbalance the inherently lonely nature of PhD work. Make sure you invest enough time in your close relationships and friendships. Carving time out to spend with others is not a 'nice to have'; it is absolutely essential for mental well-being. Making sure you establish a routine that keeps you physically active is another important choice you can make to protect your physical and mental health.
3 Worrying about whether you are competent enough to complete your PhD is normal – most candidates have those fears at some point during their PhD journey. Know that you are not alone, and that worrying about whether you are cut out for the job is normal and will pass. Making mistakes is a normal part of the process, and not a sign that you are not able to do the job.
4 Remember that you are working to put yourself in a strong position in the job market post-PhD. You are working hard to enhance your profile and give yourself the best chance at an economically prosperous future, no matter what the state of the economy might be.
5 Take shared ownership for your mental health. You have agency, but the context matters. If the university does not satisfactorily support you, speak up.

# 6 Minoritised students

## Dealing with systemic barriers and making use of EDI initiatives

### Obstacles faced by PhD students from minoritised backgrounds

Having faith in one's own abilities and staying happy, healthy, and successful during PhD study, or indeed in any other professional context, is much easier for people who do not have systemic barriers stacked against them. If you have grown up in a context where everyone treated you as if your views mattered and as if they expect you to succeed, where you are taken seriously, and where you felt key role models and teachers trusted your abilities and believed that you would naturally grow up to be successful, it is much easier to have high levels of self-belief. If, however, people treated you as if not much can be expected of you and as if certain achievements will naturally remain out of reach, then it will take a disproportionately greater amount of energy and grit to strive for those goals regardless. This is one reason why members of certain social groups, those who are more likely to not have been academically supported and encouraged in the past, struggle more. This, then, is the first obstacle for minoritised people on their academic quest. If no one told you that you could succeed, or if people told you – or implied through their behaviour – that you cannot succeed because you are from a certain background or belong to a certain social group, you might internalise this and come to believe that success is out of your reach. Teachers' expectations during formative years can lead to self-fulfilling prophecies: those students who are not expected to do well will not excel. If you do not know anyone who has ever succeeded, then attempting the challenge of a PhD will be that much more daunting. Internalised forms of self-doubt can build a psychological barrier which might prevent people from even attempting to do a PhD. A lifetime of subtle messaging around what you as a member of your group can achieve and expect will take its inevitable toll and can lead to 'internalised prejudice.' Not being supportively challenged by teachers to the same extent as students from other backgrounds can have powerful

DOI: 10.4324/9781003630074-6

impacts on educational aspirations, attainment, and outcomes, and can disadvantage members of minoritised groups.

There are also less subtle obstacles that people from minoritised backgrounds face in higher education: prejudice and discrimination undoubtedly still exist. They can present in subtle or blatant forms. If your admissions tutors and supervisors believe deep down that a PhD programme is not really a place for you, they will treat you differently, maybe offering fewer opportunities and less support, and this can obviously hinder your progress. Structural inequities may appear in admissions, grant allocation, and peer review, where implicit biases influence opportunities and outcomes.

There are, of course, other barriers too, many tangible and material: if you have to work during your studies to support yourself because your parents come from a deprived group and cannot assist you, you will have a harder time succeeding than a peer who is being bankrolled by mummy and daddy. Financial strain can be a significant challenge: stipends may be inadequate, family support limited, and some students may have additional responsibilities such as contributing to household income. Minoritised students are also often expected to take on unpaid or undervalued labour, such as mentoring or diversity-related service, which can divert time and energy from research and career development. If you have children and are a woman, you are statistically likely to pick up the lion's share of childcare and housework compared to your male peers, making it harder to dedicate the time needed to excel in your PhD. A myriad of factors can be associated with material and practical disadvantage for certain demographic groups.

So far, I have reviewed some of the main challenges faced by many students from minoritised backgrounds: lack of self-belief due to messages picked up during formative years, lack of opportunities offered due to persistent prejudice and structural barriers, and material disadvantages – for example in the form of less financial resource or a greater childcare burden. Students from minoritised backgrounds often face a complex set of challenges during PhD study that combine structural, social, and personal pressures. Underrepresentation can leave them feeling isolated or pressured to represent an entire group, while limiting access to peer support networks. Role models are powerful – to see someone 'like you' who has reached the position of Professor can be invaluable in communicating to early-career colleagues that there is a route to the top, even for someone from their background. Unfortunately, such role models are few and far between for some demographic groups.

Many minoritised students encounter hidden curricula, where unwritten rules about funding, publishing, networking, and academic advancement are less accessible to those without prior exposure, putting them at a disadvantage compared to peers from more privileged backgrounds. Implicit expectations and cultures of doctoral education may be especially opaque to those who are new to academia and unfamiliar with its cultural norms. Mentorship and advising can be particularly difficult, as students may have limited access to faculty who understand their lived experiences, which can result in unequal guidance or advocacy. Power imbalances further complicate this, since advisors often control access to resources, publications, and career pathways.

Academic climate and sense of belonging also play a major role, as students may encounter microaggressions, subtle or overt discrimination, and departmental cultures that signal that their identities or research interests are less valued. These pressures can intensify imposter feelings, chronic stress, and mental health challenges. Research constraints can add further difficulty, particularly for those studying marginalised communities, as their work may be labelled niche or less rigorous, and they may face gatekeeping in publishing or funding, alongside the emotional weight of researching topics tied to their own identities. Limited professional networks can hinder career preparation and access to post-PhD opportunities, while biases in hiring and promotion may push some students to question whether academia is a viable path.

There are a range of different demographic groups of people who suffer from systemic and historic discrimination and who have to fight harder to achieve the same outcomes. Nationwide, there are many academic achievement gaps between different ethnic groups at school and university level, disadvantaging students of Black and Afro-Caribbean backgrounds in particular. Women also face obstacles compared to men in certain subjects. Female participation in STEM subjects in particular is still low, and women still do the lion's share of the housework whilst being expected to perform at equal level with men at work, leading to a double burden to the detriment of mothers. It is also clearly harder to enter a PhD programme if you live in a disadvantaged postcode and do not have any role models to follow, nor any social network of expertise to draw on and access to people who can advise and mentor you on your journey. People who present in gender non-conformative ways face frequent discrimination, and even those who have non-native accents are discriminated against in the workplace. Not all these groups are discriminated against in society to the same extent, and it is not my intention to suggest that their suffering is equal or to pass judgement on who is facing the biggest unfair obstacles. Rather, the point is to acknowledge that higher education, and education in general, is not a level playing field, and things are easier for some students and harder for others, depending on their background.

It is also important to note that challenges are rarely isolated, and intersectional identities – such as race, gender, disability, SES, or immigration status – often amplify barriers, highlighting that these difficulties are systemic rather than individual. Despite these obstacles, many minoritised students thrive when institutions provide equitable mentorship, adequate funding, inclusive climates, and accountable structures, showing that targeted systemic support can make PhD study more accessible and sustainable for all students.

The fact that students from minority backgrounds face additional barriers at university is borne out by a number of different surveys across Europe, asking students about their lived experience compared with their peers from majority groups. Rather than evidencing overt discrimination, students often report more subtle, systemic challenges. Students commonly cite a lack of representation in curricula and teaching staff, feelings of social isolation, lower expectations from instructors, and limited access to informal networks that support academic and career progression. Financial pressures, language barriers, and experiences of microaggressions also emerge as themes affecting students' sense of belonging and overall attainment.

In response to these concerns, many European universities have increasingly recognised that inequalities cannot be addressed solely through individual support measures. Instead, there has been a shift towards examining institutional structures and cultures that may inadvertently disadvantage certain groups. One visible outcome of this shift has been the creation of senior Equality, Diversity, and Inclusion (EDI) roles, such as Pro-Vice-Chancellors, Vice-Rectors, or Directors with responsibility for EDI. By positioning these roles at a senior leadership level, universities signal that tackling systemic discrimination is a strategic priority rather than a peripheral issue. The remit of these appointments typically includes reviewing policies and practices, improving data collection on student and staff outcomes, and embedding inclusive approaches across teaching, assessment, recruitment, and promotion. Senior EDI leaders are also tasked with fostering accountability, ensuring that commitments to equity translate into measurable change. While the establishment of senior EDI posts does not, in itself, eliminate inequality, it represents an important step towards sustained institutional change.

One challenge with addressing systemic inequality is that in some countries, universities do not routinely record data on ethnicity or other demographic markers. For example, recording this information is common practice in the UK and the USA, but not in Germany. Clearly, it is difficult to track or challenge awarding gaps and other issues when there is no data. In the psychological literature on racial discrimination, a long-standing debate has been between the relative merits of colour-blind versus colour-conscious policies: in order to achieve the fairest outcomes, is it better to acknowledge 'colour' and other potential markers of disadvantage, or is it better to try to avoid 'seeing' it in order to treat everyone the same? The literature largely bears out that a colour-conscious approach is the more effective one. In the context of EDI in higher education, the clear recommendation would be for more, not less, collection of data that enables us to track systemic disadvantage.

## EDI: making the world fairer

EDI policies endorsed by many universities aim to address discrimination and unfairness that systematically disadvantage certain people and prevents them from succeeding in education and the workplace. They aim for a world where people from all backgrounds have equal opportunities and are equally represented. In the UK, EDI is grounded in the Equality Act 2010, which places duties on universities and employers to prevent discrimination, advance equality of opportunity, and foster good relations between groups. The fact that certain groups of students are still, to this day, facing more obstacles to enter and to succeed at postgraduate education is ironic, because many in positions of power in higher education see themselves as liberal, enlightened, and supportive of an egalitarian environment. Sadly, those ideals are not yet always aligned with the reality on the ground. This is simply not good enough, and we must do better. Indeed, there is now growing awareness of this as an enormous problem in higher education, and in recent years many EDI initiatives have been designed to tackle these types of issues. This is, of course, a very welcome development, although the problems are too deep seated to expect quick changes.

I would encourage you as a prospective PhD student from a minority background to be sure to make use of any EDI initiatives that are open to you. Many universities, in recognition of the greater barriers faced by some, put programmes and support systems into place in an attempt to level the playing field. These can be aimed at reducing awarding gaps, making sure that those from minoritised backgrounds feel welcome and are aware of opportunities, or they can entail material support such as studentships earmarked for applicants from certain demographic groups. Where EDI opportunities do not exist, it is a legitimate question to ask why not and to advocate for them.

One problem with EDI initiatives is that those who benefit from them sometimes feel, unnecessarily, that they have not 'earned' their achievements and that they have somehow 'cheated.' I know women who were upset about being congratulated for being the first woman to receive a certain honour, because they felt it diminished the achievement and implied that they had not been honoured on the basis of equal merit but on the basis of their gender. I have also seen Black students who worried that their scholarship earmarked for Black students would be seen as less prestigious than a 'normal' scholarship. Therefore, it is incredibly important to be clear that EDI initiatives are not designed to give disadvantaged students an unfair 'leg up.' They are designed to fight a deep-seated, unfair, historic disadvantage. They are designed to make the world fairer. They are not advantaging minoritised students, they are – if implemented successfully – stopping them from being unfairly disadvantaged.

In sum, PhD work entails many challenges even for those students from privileged backgrounds. For those from minoritised backgrounds, additional hurdles of internalised prejudice, actual prejudice encountered at university, and manifest material obstacles can make the situation even more challenging. Be aware that things are not difficult because you are incompetent or an imposter, but because there are objective challenges that make it harder for you. Make use of EDI initiatives where they are offered and demand more support where it is not in place.

Nonetheless, some commentators have questioned whether EDI initiatives, whilst undoubtedly useful for disadvantaged individuals, are a source of social cohesion or fragmentation when considered at a more systemic level. The objectives of EDI, most academics would agree, are inarguably sound from a moral or ethical standpoint. The world *should* be fair for all, and we should work towards this aim. Yet, what is right and wrong in the implementation of EDI principles is often controversial, and in some countries, there has recently been a political backlash against EDI.

Some have argued that the focus on identity-based divisions (such as those on the basis of race, gender, or sexuality) can undermine a sense of shared belonging and erode the social glue. According to this view, EDI fosters division by emphasising differences rather than shared goals, potentially creating resentment or tokenism. A counterargument is, of course, that it is entirely possible to identify with subgroups and an overarching common identity simultaneously.

Concerns also centre on a belief that these programmes prioritise identity over merit. Critics argue that EDI can lead to hiring, promotion, or admissions decisions based on race, gender, or other characteristics rather than qualifications or achievement, which they claim undermines fairness and excellence. Some see EDI as promoting 'reverse discrimination,' where individuals from majority or traditionally privileged groups are unfairly disadvantaged. There are also objections that mandatory training or quotas can be bureaucratic, performative, or inefficient, without producing measurable improvements in outcomes. In essence, the central objection is that EDI, while aiming to address structural inequities, risks compromising meritocratic principles and individual assessment, leading some to question whether such initiatives truly advance organisational effectiveness or social justice.

Another interesting question concerns the relationship between group-based and individual-based interventions. At the individual level, 'reasonable adjustments' (e.g., flexible hours, mental health accommodations) are the typical mechanism to achieve equity. Such adjustments are based on the recognition that people have diverse needs and that equal treatment isn't always fair treatment. Occupational health adjustments are focused on individuals and EDI is focused on justice for groups, but in practice many needs for reasonable adjustments might arise to avoid systemic discrimination against certain groups, for example those with disabilities. Reasonable adjustments work in environments that are resource-rich, where the needs of a individuals can easily be accommodated. But the accommodation can be at the expense of the group: if one person works less, others have to work more. If one person cannot give the Monday morning lecture, another person will have to stand in. In environments that are resource poor, or where a majority of individuals request a host of different accommodations, this can become difficult or impossible to manage if resources are so tight that the needs of the individual and the group (or other individuals in that group) are in uncomfortable competition. The question of 'fairness' then becomes deeply political and contested.

Maybe most importantly, EDI has sometimes been presented as being pitted against Freedom of Speech (FoS) legislation. The UK Higher Education (Freedom of Speech) Act 2023 protects open debate and prevents unlawful suppression of views in universities. It strengthens rights to express lawful views without institutional penalty and introduces duties for universities and student unions to protect academic freedom, allow a diversity of speakers, and avoid 'no-platforming' except where speech would be unlawful (e.g., harassment, incitement, or discrimination). Tensions can arise where there is a perception that EDI initiatives can encourage limiting speech that may be experienced as harmful or exclusionary, while FoS legislation emphasises protecting robust debate even when opinions cause discomfort. Critics of EDI have argued that this embeds a political stance into institutional policy. However, the normative values behind EDI – fairness, equal opportunity, and inclusion – are not partisan but compliant with anti-discrimination law and the duty to ensure equitable access and fair treatment. Nonetheless, political contestation arises around how EDI is implemented, not whether equality should be upheld. In practice, universities must balance both duties: EDI should not be used to suppress lawful speech, and FoS should not be used to legitimise discriminatory behaviour.

The Office for Students (OfS), as the regulator of higher education in England, has been clear that universities are not spaces in which students have a right to avoid offence (as of the time of writing). In its guidance on FoS and academic freedom, the OfS acknowledges that higher education can involve engagement with contested, provocative, and sometimes unsettling ideas. While universities have duties to ensure lawful speech and student welfare, feeling offended or uncomfortable is not, in itself, a harm that institutions are required to prevent. Rather, exposure to challenging lawful viewpoints is intrinsic to the academic endeavour. Universities exist to test assumptions, interrogate evidence, and develop students' capacity for critical reasoning. This process cannot occur if ideas are filtered according to whether they align with prevailing moral, political, or cultural sensibilities. Being confronted with arguments one disagrees with encourages students to clarify their own positions, identify weaknesses in their reasoning, and develop intellectual resilience. Learning to tolerate discomfort is therefore not an incidental by-product of higher education but a core educational outcome. Preparing students for exposure to unsettling ideas equips them not only for academic success but also for professional and civic life, where disagreement and ambiguity are unavoidable. Intellectual growth depends on the ability to listen, analyse, and respond to ideas that challenge one's worldview. This view honours students as emerging adults who are capable of – and need to be supported in their journey towards – engaging robustly with complexity and controversy, rather than as consumers entitled to emotional comfort.

I believe that the importance of exposure to opposing views extends beyond individual development to the health of society as a whole, a point that can be illuminated through Gordon Allport's intergroup contact theory. Allport argued that prejudice is reduced when individuals have meaningful contact with those they perceive as different, particularly under conditions of equal status, shared goals, cooperation, and institutional support. While his theory was developed in relation to social groups, its logic applies to the realm of ideas and beliefs. When people are insulated from opposing viewpoints, disagreement is easily caricatured, and outgroups – whether ideological, cultural, or political – are seen as irrational or threatening. Universities can provide structured environments in which students encounter rival perspectives in ways that encourage dialogue rather than hostility. Exposure to disagreement, when guided by norms of reasoned debate and mutual respect, helps individuals recognise complexity and common humanity across divides. This reduces the tendency to moralise difference and fosters habits of listening and compromise. From a societal perspective, such intellectual contact is essential for cohesion in pluralistic democracies, where citizens must coexist despite deep disagreements. Allport's theory suggests that avoidance of opposing views entrenches polarisation, while engagement – though often uncomfortable – builds understanding and trust. Universities therefore play a crucial civic role: by habituating students to sustained engagement with difference, they help cultivate citizens capable of navigating disagreement without retreating into antagonism or exclusion.

Despite debates over the ways in which EDI principles might concretely be implemented, and the sometimes uneasy relationship between EDI perspectives and legislation on free speech, it is undeniably positive that organisations examine how access and success can be more equitable and freer from discrimination. By addressing systemic barriers, EDI initiatives help create a fairer environment where talent can thrive regardless of background. Combined with meaningful engagement, adequate resources, and transparent evaluation, we can be hopeful that higher education EDI initiatives will reduce barriers for minority students and create more inclusive and equitable university environments. If you are eligible to benefit from such programmes – whether through mentorship, funding, or support networks – it is sensible to take advantage of them. Using these opportunities does not diminish merit; rather, it allows you to navigate a system historically shaped by inequality, levelling the playing field and enabling your skills and potential to be fully realised.

## Experiences of members of minoritised groups during PhD study – insights from interviews with recent PhD students

When thinking about systemic discrimination in higher education, I did not want to stop at reading theoretical accounts of it. Being conscious of the different backgrounds of my own students, I was motivated to understand how the issue 'feels' in their own lived experience. My own experience of doing a PhD is undoubtedly shaped by my gender. Wanting to understand the lived experience of students who face other and potentially larger structural barriers, I interviewed a few of my current and former PhD students and asked them to share their experiences of doing a PhD as a member of a minoritised group. These were semi-structured interviews, covering examples where my students felt their group membership informed how they were treated, the obstacles they encountered because of their identity, and measures they thought would be helpful in supporting minoritised people during their PhD study. Responses were transcribed and analysed with thematic analysis. Students had a range of different minoritised identities related to their ethnicity, first-gen/working class background, immigrant/refugee status or international student status, accent, gender, and sexual identity. Below, I will summarise the themes that emerged from these interviews. Many of them tally with what has been summarised above, but the students' descriptions undoubtedly add more depth and colour.

Overall, my students communicated a strong 'Awareness of Minority Identity and Representation.' They reported a strong awareness of their minority identity, often feeling a heightened sense of responsibility to perform well: 'You are being expected to be excellent… I can't let the people down that have made this possible.' Being part of a small minority group in academia contributed to increased self-awareness: 'There's not very many people that fit … into that category.' This awareness often came with a sense of pride and motivation to inspire others: 'I can hopefully make it possible for people coming behind me to feel like … they can do this as well.' Identity salience was also reported as context dependent. Some identities, particularly those that could be concealed, required more mental effort due to impression management, whereas visible identities were less cognitively demanding – for identities that are clearly 'out there', no cognitive effort needs to be spent on managing appearances because they are taken as a given. Students noted differences in comfort and acceptance depending on the environment: 'At PhD level… I feel very comfortable … at undergraduate level there were some pangs when hearing people talk about [identity category].' Even in supportive environments, there was continued awareness of potential subtle biases and experiences of imposter syndrome: 'The imposter syndrome is definitely … part of coming from [minoritised group].'

My students also communicated very clearly about being aware of 'Intersectionality and Compounded Identities.' They described managing multiple minoritised identities, with context influencing which aspects of their identity became salient: 'It depends on which space I'm in … different aspects of my identity come to the fore.' Some aspects of their identity could confer privilege, highlighting the importance of agency even within marginalised groups: 'Because I am well-spoken, people do treat me differently … that is perhaps a privilege I am aware of.'

Another theme that emerged was related to the 'hidden curriculum' experience mentioned above; this was a theme around 'Limited Access to Opportunities and Knowledge Gaps.' Students referred to a lack of information and guidance about academic opportunities. Students often had to 'do [their] own digging' to find scholarships, PhD pathways, or networking opportunities: 'I had no idea that these opportunities are available … sometimes it feels like you have to do your own digging.' Early support, mentorship, and guidance were seen as essential to successfully navigating academia: 'If I had not been offered this [EDI-initiative related] support, none of this would have been as easily available to me.'

Another theme summarised a range of different 'Challenges in Academia,' as experienced by my students from minoritised backgrounds. They reported multiple challenges, including navigating hidden rules, lack of mentorship, financial pressures, and systemic biases. Mentorship and guidance were seen as critical to career progression: 'You need someone to talk to you about it, because otherwise you might not find that stuff or you might not realise that that is important.' Financial obstacles were cited as something that could make PhD study difficult: 'It was like £800 something pounds a month … without the teaching work, I'm not sure I would have been able to do the PhD anyway.' Imposter syndrome and exclusion were common: 'The imposter syndrome is definitely … part of coming from [minoritised group].' It was also noted that traditional metrics can disadvantage minoritised students, highlighting the importance of recognising potential: 'Understanding that there's a difference between potential and the opportunities you see on someone's CV … you'd rather look at potential more rather than only judging by … the sorts of traditional metrics.' Finally, students emphasised the need to avoid overgeneralising experiences: 'Not conflating … the difference between being a black British student versus an international student … very different experiences … don't lump people into the same boat because of their ethnicity.'

One theme that emerged was around 'Positives of Minority Identity in Academia.' Despite challenges, minoritised students highlighted the advantages of their perspective: 'Maybe I'm able to see things and contribute in a way that I might not if I didn't think about this because of who I am.' They also valued their ability to inspire others and act as role models:

I was also interested in my students' views on how support for those from disadvantaged backgrounds should ideally be offered. The last theme, therefore, clustered around 'Recommendations for Supporting Minoritised Students.' Students emphasised several mechanisms to support minoritised students: First, mentorship and peer support were mentioned: 'Just having access to people who have some of their experiences … just to be able to talk about whatever it is that they want to talk about.' Second, inclusive practices and visible signals were emphasised: 'Visible signs like "you're welcome here" … this is a space for you … please engage.' Third, challenging assumptions and staff training were seen as important: 'Training staff … challenge those assumptions is really important and then actually challenging those assumptions in the PhD cohort as well.' Fourth, there was a recommendation by the students to focus on potential over credentials: 'You'd rather look at potential more rather than only judging by … traditional metrics … that doesn't necessarily tell you how good they're going to be.' Fifth, financial and structural support were unsurprisingly mentioned: 'Without the teaching work, I'm not sure I would have been able to do the PhD anyway.' Sixth, an inclusive understanding of disadvantage was encouraged: 'The biggest factor actually … wasn't ethnicity. It was coming from a first-gen working class background … that is often overlooked by EDI initiatives.'

Last but not least, my students were keen to note the positive as well as the negative and to communicate an optimistic outlook and problem-solving attitude. The last theme, therefore, was around a 'Positive Outlook and Improvements Over Time.' They recognised improvements in academic inclusion over time: 'Even I can remember things being worse … and I can definitely see how things have changed enormously over the last 20–30 years … we're kind of getting there.'

## Gender and achievement in higher education

As mentioned, my own PhD experience was a gendered one. Although gender may not pose the biggest barrier to academic success, it does merit special attention because of the large number of women who enter university (a slightly larger proportion than men in the UK, nationwide) and the relatively small number of women who succeed in making it into the top academic positions. What's going on with this dynamic? In the UK and many other countries, there is a curious effect whereby women are in a slight majority among the undergraduate student population and are roughly equally represented (averaging across all disciplines) in the PhD population, but are in the minority among academic staff, especially at the more senior professor level. This pattern has been termed a 'leaky pipeline' – the attrition occurs after entry, not before. What might be contributing factors? A whole range of variables influence this effect.

For starters, there is often differential encouragement towards PhD-level study based on gender bias. Then, there are structural reasons for why women might have it harder during their PhD (and afterwards within academia) compared to male peers. I will highlight four of the main ones here. Academia strives towards excellence, which is measured in metrics such as impact factors, numbers of publications, and grant income. Because women still take on a disproportionate portion of the caring burden (for children, elderly relatives, household chores), they have more competing demands on their time, which disadvantages them in optimising their performance on these indices. Essentially, women are judged by standards that disadvantage them, and a system that is allegedly built on meritocracy is in fact gender biased.

Moreover, some data suggests that women are more often asked to assume – and volunteer to take on or at least do not as forcefully push back against – work within academia that is necessary but that does not map onto promotion criteria. Women often disproportionally contribute to internal self-governance, mentorship, student recruitment activities, and so on. All these activities are necessary, but they do not lead to career advancement to the same degree as a stellar paper or significant grant capture. Male colleagues, who tend to be more protective of their time and more likely to hit the latter crucial metrics, end up better off. PhD students are socialised into an academic environment where women end up with additional career obstacles.

Another factor that might contribute to gender bias is that the things that get rewarded in academia are in themselves gendered. The most successful academics, the ones that are known beyond the boundaries of their narrow discipline and remembered for decades or generations, tend to be charismatic individuals (charisma itself being a gendered concept) who are visionary and outstanding thought leaders. This psychological profile is the exact opposite to the societal female ideal of being modest, collaborative, supportive of others rather than solitarily seeking the limelight. Academia rewards big ideas and big egos more than supportive and collaborative work, and the tension between what gets rewarded and societal expectations about female behaviour is another factor that contributes to gender bias.

Last but not least, pursuing a PhD with a suitable supervisor and successfully securing a PostDoc position afterwards often require geographic mobility and the acceptance of short-term contracts. This poses structural obstacles for women more than for men – women with small children, or women aspiring to have children, are less likely to accept those conditions than men. There is good evidence that children also hinder female academic career progression – the gender pay gap observed at many universities is noticeably diminished for women without children. There is a clear career penalty for women who choose to have families. This does not mean that having a family and successfully completing a PhD, or successfully navigating an academic career, are incompatible goals. Many women manage to combine both types of demands. It does mean, however, that there are structural factors that make this harder for women compared to male peers. This puts a sobering question mark over the notion that women these days really can 'have it all.' There are now initiatives designed to address some of these biases, such as the Athena Swan badging offered by Advance HE, a UK-based higher education charity. This is endorsed by many universities. Unfortunately, such exercises always bear the danger of dissolving into tick-box exercises rather than initiatives that can bring about real change. In any case, although we have undoubtedly come a long way, there is still a long way to go to achieve true gender equality in higher education.

## The important role of allyship and solidarity

As a social psychologist who has published on the psychology of prejudice, discrimination, intergroup relations, allyship, and solidarity, I can't resist adding some reflections on how people from non-minoritised backgrounds can contribute to making higher education a more inclusive place. The analysis of data to unearth inequality and the implementation of policies to address them are important. But, what is also important are the thousands of interpersonal interactions we have across group divides on an almost daily basis and the important signalling functions those can have. They can serve to humanise or dehumanise, to foster a feeling of inclusion or exclusion, and therefore contribute to the constant drip-drip-drip that informs the experience and outcomes of those from minoritised backgrounds.

Allyship and solidarity are critical to the success of minoritised PhD students because doctoral study is not only an intellectual endeavour, but also a deeply social and psychological one. Social psychology shows that belongingness is a fundamental human need; when students feel marginalised or invisible in academic spaces, their motivation, well-being, and persistence suffer. Allyship from supervisors, peers, and institutions helps counteract this by signalling that minoritised students are valued and legitimate members of the academic community. Such solidarity can be communicated, for example, via the absence of microaggressions and exclusions, via explicit and overt invitations for inclusion, or via the use of symbols – for example, my university encourages employees to wear a lanyard displaying the LGBT+ community rainbow flag.

The positive effects of feeling included despite once's group membership have been demonstrated in a range of different psychological research fields. Research on stereotype threat demonstrates that awareness of negative stereotypes can impair performance and confidence. For example, simply making people aware of their group memberships, where those are aligned with stereotypes of underperformance, can have a measurable detrimental effect on test performance. The flipside of this is that communicating that students or peers are expected to succeed will have positive effects. Effective allies actively affirm competence and create environments where minoritised scholars are not treated as representatives of their group but as complex individuals. This reduces cognitive load and allows students to focus on research rather than self-protection.

Similarly, social identity theory highlights that positive recognition of one's identity strengthens self-esteem and engagement. People are motivated towards achieving or maintaining positive self-esteem, and this is essential for academic performance because it supports motivation, resilience, and students' willingness to engage with challenges and persist after setbacks. Research evidence supports a consistent reciprocal association between higher self-esteem and better academic outcomes. Moreover, there is strong evidence that people draw a large part of their self-esteem from their membership in social groups, and if a minoritised student is denied the privilege of positive self-esteem because of negative messaging about the social group they belong to, this has evident detrimental consequences for academic ambition and achievement. Acts of solidarity, via communicating respect and inclusion, make for a supportive environment that will benefit minoritised students.

Moreover, a growth mindset, as proposed by Carol Dweck, emphasises that abilities and intelligence can be developed through effort, effective strategies, and support. Promoting this mindset can be particularly valuable for students from minoritised backgrounds, who may face systemic barriers or internalise stereotypes about their academic potential. By fostering the belief that challenges are opportunities for learning rather than reflections of innate ability, educators can help these students build resilience and confidence in their academic capabilities. This approach also encourages a more inclusive classroom culture, where mistakes are treated as part of the learning process and all students' contributions are valued. When teachers explicitly praise effort, strategy, and progress rather than innate talent, students from underrepresented groups are more likely to feel that their growth is recognised and supported. Embedding a growth mindset can counteract stereotype threat and create an environment in which all students feel included and capable of success.

Solidarity among peers and mentors also fosters collective efficacy – the shared belief that challenges can be overcome together. Peer networks provide emotional validation, practical guidance, and models of success that counter isolation. Crucially, allyship must be active rather than symbolic: listening, advocating, redistributing opportunities, and challenging inequitable norms. When embedded structurally and interpersonally, allyship and solidarity transform the PhD from an isolating trial into a sustainable, empowering journey for minoritised scholars and a more enriching and rewarding learning experience for all students, regardless of their background.

## Professional societies and EDI – the British Psychological Society (BPS) as an example

There are many professional societies relevant to higher education which make concerted efforts to grapple with the issues of fair access to opportunities, knowledge, and routes to success. To give an example, as a psychologist myself I shall briefly outline the approach taken by the professional organisation most relevant to my own field: the BPS. The following was accurate at the time of writing, but as with any policy, this will be under continuous review and might be subject to change in the future. The BPS centres EDI in its mission to promote rigorous and socially responsible psychology. Its Declaration on EDI commits the society to building a culture of equal opportunity and embedding EDI values across governance and membership. A dedicated EDI Board drives policy, monitors progress, and assesses both internal practices and the BPS's wider professional role. The BPS collects diversity data to identify underrepresented groups, target actions, and evaluate the impact of interventions. It also works with the Academy of Social Sciences to acknowledge psychology's historical injustices, including discriminatory uses of IQ testing, using this understanding to guide a fairer future. EDI is framed as practice as well as policy: resources such as the teachers' toolkit and clinical supervision guidance emphasise inclusive environments and attention to identity, diversity, and power. At the same time, the BPS cautions that unconscious bias training has limited evidence of long-term effects and argues for structural, measurable EDI objectives instead. In its 2024 Strategy, the BPS makes EDI a core priority and pledges to 'embed EDI and ensure access for all.' While recent commitments include stronger governance, data collection, and curriculum reform, critics argue progress is slow and uneven. The ongoing challenge is turning EDI ambitions into systemic, sustained change.

In the context of this book, the stance of professional societies such as the BPS on EDI is relevant, because the society accredits PhD-level training programmes and thereby informs how EDI issues are embedded (or not) in doctoral study. In its Standards for Accreditation for doctoral programmes (e.g., Clinical Psychology), the BPS explicitly requires that programmes have 'equality, diversity and inclusion policies.' In the Alternative Handbook (a BPS guide for doctoral clinical psychology trainees), there is explicit discussion of EDI: the 2025–2026 edition includes survey data on trainees and mentions that EDI is a priority in training and selection. The Clinical Psychology Forum has published work on how trainee clinical psychologists understand racial equity and decolonisation within their DClinPsy training. For Educational Psychology doctorates, the BPS also notes that the 'ways in which education providers implement their equality, diversity, and inclusion … policies' are part of quality accreditation. Moreover, according to BPS supervision guidance, supervisors (including for trainees doing doctoral work) should engage with 'difference, intersectionality and EDI … and their implications for working practices.' There is growing recognition of the importance of culturally responsive supervision: BPS-published trainee perspectives suggest that supervision which takes account of cultural background, identity, and power can improve the supervisory relationship and outcomes. What is more, the BPS encourages programmes to reflect on racial equity and decolonisation. In sum, the BPS sees EDI as deeply relevant to doctoral training. It mandates EDI in accreditation, expects supervisors to be sensitive to identity and power, supports culturally responsive supervision, and is pushing for racial equity and decolonisation in training. Importantly, it also recognises the systemic barriers that affect doctoral trainees and seeks to address them through research, policy, and support structures.

The BPS is far from alone in putting EDI centre stage. UKRI, the major national funder of doctoral training, frames EDI as essential to research excellence and responsible funding practice. Doctoral Training Partnerships (DTPs) and Centres for Doctoral Training (CDTs) must demonstrate robust EDI strategies as a condition of funding. This includes evidence of fair recruitment, interventions to address underrepresentation, data-driven monitoring, and mechanisms to tackle harassment and bullying. UKRI requires institutions to produce annual EDI action plans, monitor participation through demographic data, and show 'meaningful progress' in diversifying doctoral cohorts. The emphasis is on system-level change, equitable access to research careers, and addressing structural inequalities in the research environment.

Such conscious tackling of systemic barriers and attention to issues related to inequalities can be important agents of change to achieve a fairer future for all. Although we are a long way from a world where access to and success in PhD-level study is truly a level playing field, important progress has been made. To be sure, we would not want to go back to a world where the advantage of white, middle-class men is unquestioningly taken for granted as the societal norm and status quo.

To summarise the themes that emerge from this review, Table 6.1 presents the main barriers, causes, and potential solutions to minoritised student PhD success. We have made progress, but there is more work to do to ensure that higher education becomes a true level playing field.

*Table 6.1* Barriers, causes, and solutions to minoritised student success

| *Barrier* | *Underlying causes* | *Potential solutions/supports* |
|---|---|---|
| **Low self-belief, imposter syndrome, and internalised prejudice** | Negative or low expectations from teachers and society during formative years; lack of encouragement; absence of role models; self-fulfilling prophecies | Early encouragement and high expectations; visible role models; mentorship programmes; reassurance that barriers are systemic, not individual failings |
| **Prejudice and discrimination (overt and subtle)** | Persistent societal biases; implicit bias in admissions, supervision, funding, and peer review; discriminatory attitudes towards accents, gender expression, race, or identity | Bias-aware recruitment and assessment; staff training; accountability structures; transparent decision-making |

(*Continued*)

*Table 6.1* (Continued)

| *Barrier* | *Underlying causes* | *Potential solutions/supports* |
|---|---|---|
| **Structural inequities in access to opportunities** | Hidden curricula around funding, publishing, and networking; reliance on informal knowledge networks; power imbalances with supervisors | Explicit guidance on academic pathways; transparent communication of opportunities; structured mentoring and advising |
| **Financial hardship and material disadvantage** | Inadequate stipends; lack of family financial support; need for paid work alongside study; socioeconomic background | Targeted studentships; bursaries; paid teaching opportunities; cost-of-living support |
| **Unequal caring and domestic responsibilities** | Gendered expectations around childcare and housework; lack of flexible working norms; limited institutional support | Flexible working arrangements; parental leave policies; childcare support; recognition of caring responsibilities |
| **Excess unpaid or undervalued labour** | Expectations that minoritised students contribute to diversity work, mentoring, or service without recognition | Workload monitoring; recognition and reward for service work; redistribution of labour |
| **Isolation and underrepresentation** | Low numbers of minoritised students and staff; lack of peer support networks; pressure to represent an entire group | Cohort-building initiatives; peer support groups; visible commitment to inclusion |
| **Limited access to culturally responsive mentorship** | Few supervisors with shared or understood lived experiences; unequal advocacy | Culturally responsive supervision; mentor matching; multiple-mentor models |
| **Hostile or exclusionary academic climates** | Microaggressions; departmental cultures that devalue certain identities or research topics | Inclusive departmental practices; visible signals of belonging; clear reporting mechanisms |
| **Devaluation of research on marginalised communities** | Gatekeeping in publishing and funding; perceptions of work as 'niche' or less rigorous | Broader definitions of academic excellence; inclusive evaluation criteria |

(*Continued*)

*Table 6.1* (Continued)

| *Barrier* | *Underlying causes* | *Potential solutions/supports* |
|---|---|---|
| **Bias in traditional metrics of excellence** | Overreliance on publications, grants, and prestige pathways that favour privileged groups | Holistic assessment focusing on potential as well as achievement |
| **Intersectional and compounded disadvantage** | Overlapping identities (e.g., race, gender, class, disability, immigration status) amplifying barriers | Intersectional EDI strategies; inclusive definitions of disadvantage |
| **Barriers to progression and retention (e.g., 'leaky pipeline' for women)** | Gender bias in evaluation; caring burdens; geographic mobility requirements; short-term contracts | Structural reforms; flexible career pathways; gender equity initiatives (e.g., Athena Swan) |
| **Fear of stigma around EDI support** | Perception that EDI initiatives undermine merit; internalised narratives of 'unearned' success | Clear communication that EDI addresses historic disadvantage; normalisation of support usage |
| **Limited professional networks and career preparation** | Restricted access to informal networks; bias in hiring and promotion | Networking support; career development programmes; fair hiring practices |

## Top tips

1 Recognise that structural barriers are real – and they are not a reflection of your ability. If your PhD feels harder than it seems to be for others, this does not mean you are less capable. Systemic disadvantage, hidden curricula, and historic inequities make the path steeper for some students. Struggling is often not evidence of personal inadequacy; it is often evidence of unfair conditions.

2 Actively seek out role models, mentors, and information – even when it feels difficult. Access to informal knowledge about funding, publishing, and career progression is uneven. You may need support in addition to 'doing your own digging,' but you are not asking for special treatment – you are compensating for an uneven playing field. Mentorship and peer support can make a decisive difference.

3 Make use of EDI initiatives without guilt or self-doubt. Equity-based support is not about giving you an unfair advantage; it exists to counter historic and ongoing disadvantage. Accepting this support does not diminish your merit or achievements – it allows your ability and potential to be properly recognised.

4 Protect your well-being and sense of belonging. Isolation, microaggressions, and pressure to represent an entire group can take a cumulative toll. Investing time in supportive relationships, affirming spaces, and physical and mental health is not optional – it is essential for sustaining yourself through the PhD.
5 Speak up where systems fall short, and remember that change is collective. You have agency, but responsibility does not rest on individuals alone. Universities and supervisors have obligations to create fair, inclusive environments. When support is missing, it is legitimate to ask why and to advocate, individually or collectively, for better structures.

# 7 International students

## Additional pointers

Chapter 2 has already covered some of the key admissions-related issues that international students wanting to study for a PhD at British universities must be aware of. These will not be reiterated here, but a brief reminder of some of the key issues will be given. For international students considering a PhD in the UK, thorough planning and awareness of the process are essential. The journey begins with identifying research interests and potential supervisors. Unlike some countries where structured programmes dominate, UK PhDs are often research-focused, so students are expected to approach a supervisor whose research aligns with their own. Reviewing faculty profiles, reading recent publications, and directly contacting prospective supervisors with a tailored research proposal are often essential for securing acceptance. Your first job is to find the right person, and your second job is to persuade this person to champion you and assist you in the admissions process. The future supervisor will often be of great assistance in explaining the admissions criteria and steps, and in strengthening any research proposal and application documents by providing feedback. Building a strong allyship with a potential supervisor is a major step towards eventual success.

International students should consider admission requirements before approaching potential supervisors. UK universities typically require a strong academic record, usually a Master's degree in a relevant field, although exceptional candidates may be accepted with a bachelor's degree. Proof of English proficiency through tests like IELTS or TOEFL is usually mandatory for non-native speakers, unless the previous language of instruction was English. Additionally, some programmes may request prior research experience, publications, or references from academic mentors.

Funding is a crucial consideration. UK PhDs can be costly, and international students often face higher tuition fees than domestic students. Funding options include university scholarships, research council studentships, or external grants. Some students also explore assistantships or part-time work, though visa restrictions limit the hours international

DOI: 10.4324/9781003630074-7

students can work. Careful planning of finances is vital, including estimating living costs, tuition, and healthcare contributions. Ideally, students bring funding in the form of a scholarship from their home country (yes, more easily said than done). Such funding can also go a long way in persuading potential supervisors to invest in you, so if you have funding in place, make sure you communicate this in your first approach. If you do not yet have funding in place but have an overall strong academic profile, the future supervisor can be an invaluable source of information regarding what funding opportunities exist from sources in the destination country.

Visa requirements represent another important consideration. Prospective students must secure a UK student visa, which requires an unconditional offer from a recognised university, proof of sufficient funds, and sometimes additional documentation. The visa process is lengthy, so early preparation and starting early are advisable. Accommodation and settling into life in the UK are practical considerations that should not be overlooked. University-provided housing or private rentals can be arranged in advance, and familiarising yourself with local transport, healthcare, and banking systems eases the transition.

Finally, planning the research itself is critical. Typically, this is done by drafting a research proposal which is then further refined and developed by input from your potential supervisor, once you have secured buy-in from them. You will need a strong initial proposal in order to generate interest, but also be able to demonstrate strong time management, project planning, and academic writing skills. In summary, international students aiming to pursue a PhD in the UK will need to focus on identifying suitable programmes, meeting admission criteria, securing funding, navigating visa processes, and planning their research strategy. Early preparation and proactive engagement are essential for a successful PhD journey in the UK.

A last crucial aspect of transitioning into your PhD studies concerns preparation for cultural and practical adjustments. Cultural adaptation is key, as international students may face differences in teaching style, research expectations, and social norms. The challenges posed by navigating a new culture and unfamiliar education system – as well as ways to navigating them – are worth reflecting on. Transnational education and cross-cultural experiences can provide some of the most enriching impulses for personal, academic, professional, and even spiritual growth. Yet, the cultural transition is not always easy.

Culture shock can be experienced in relation to the way people relate to each other – what is seen as normative and non-offensive in interpersonal communication often differs between different cultures. But it can also relate to other aspects of the environment or to how things work, in a more general sense. Over the years, my students have pointed out a number of things they found peculiar about British culture. A few that stuck in my mind were: astonishment at how little time there is, given that most Brits do not have household help to take care of many mundane tasks (cooking, washing, cleaning) as would be customary in many middle-class homes in some countries; complaints about the cold and lack of sunlight; confusion about displays of mass drunkenness in town centres on a Saturday night; incredulousness that some Brits tend to walk around in T-shirts even in the height of winter; and the orderliness of a British queue. However, many of the most challenging aspects of cross-cultural transition relate to what is expected and seen as desirable when people talk to each other, and I will elaborate on some examples in the following.

## The perils of cross-cultural communication

What is important whilst doing a PhD as well as in the workplace more generally is an ability to work well with others, to motivate others, and to manage conflict and disagreements in a constructive way. Tremendously useful is not only a high IQ – the generalised level of cognitive intelligence – but also a high EQ – 'emotional intelligence.' This is the ability to be aware of, control, and appropriately express one's emotions. It is the ability to read and understand other people and to infer their state of mind from their signals and behaviour, which is a prerequisite for handling interpersonal relationships judiciously and empathetically. In short, 'emotional intelligence' is what allows you to 'get on' with people. However, the potential for miscommunication and misunderstandings arises when communicating across cultural boundaries, even for those who score high on EQ. Both subtle nonverbal cues and verbal cues can easily be misunderstood in cross-cultural settings. Signals that mean one thing in one culture mean something entirely different in another culture. For example, the statement 'I am not entirely sure I agree with this' can be indicative of strong criticism and objection if voiced by a British person, whereas the same words uttered by a German are likely to only indicate uncertainty. It is therefore important that international PhD students, and those supervising them, stay alert to the potential of cross-cultural misunderstandings and be ready to troubleshoot when they arise. It is also important to be careful to be charitable in one's attributions and explanations of other people's behaviours: rather than jumping to conclusions that someone is rude, thoughtless, difficult, it is always worth considering whether discomfort experienced in cross-cultural communication might be due to different cultural norms, rather than due to malicious intent on the part of the other.

Academia and the world of PhD students, especially in Anglophone settings, are incredibly multicultural and diverse. For example, in my own department I have colleagues from over 20 different countries. And this is just among the staff; the student body is even more diverse. This level of diversity is quite common in UK universities, and this puts into sharp relief the need to be mindful of the potential for cross-cultural misunderstandings. The types of misunderstandings that might arise are as diverse as there are cultural idiosyncrasies; in other words, the list is endless. I have witnessed issues arise due to different cultural norms of how bluntly, directly, and forcefully arguments should be presented. Without wanting to rehash overgeneralised cultural stereotypes, the British approach to conflict resolution in the case of differences of opinion is often more subtle than, for example, the German, Dutch, or Israeli approach. I have also witnessed issues caused by diverging cultural norms related to physical contact between people and comfortable standing distance between individuals (generally quite restraint/contact avoidant in the British culture, certainly more tactile in other cultures).

Navigating cross-cultural communication requires awareness, adaptability, and active listening. The first step is developing cultural sensitivity: understand that norms, values, and communication styles differ across cultures, and avoid assuming your approach is universal. Active listening is crucial – pay attention not just to words but to tone, body language, and context, as meanings can vary widely. Ask clarifying questions politely when unsure, and be patient with misunderstandings. Flexibility in communication style helps; for example, some cultures value directness, while others prioritise harmony and indirect expression. Avoid stereotyping, and treat each interaction as unique. Building rapport through small talk, showing respect for customs, and being mindful of nonverbal cues can foster trust. Finally, reflect on your own cultural biases and adapt accordingly, creating an environment where open, respectful, and effective communication can flourish across cultural boundaries. The list of potential ways in which cultural differences can lead to misunderstandings is endless. I will flesh out two further examples to illustrate what dynamics can arise due to cultural differences.

## Cross-cultural differences at the application stage: an East-West example

Cultural differences significantly influence how students approach learning and the expression of original thought. In some educational cultures, particularly in Western contexts, students are encouraged to question, critique, and propose their own ideas, with teachers acting as facilitators rather than sole authorities. In contrast, in many other cultures, learning is more hierarchical, and students are expected to respect the teacher's expertise, often prioritising memorisation and correct answers over independent thinking. These differences can affect classroom participation, academic confidence, and assessment approaches. Recognising and bridging these expectations is crucial for international students adapting to new educational environments.

The same cultural differences described above can also lead to misunderstandings in the initial application stage when you first communicate with potential supervisors, potentially causing obstacles already at the first hurdle. As mentioned above, in the UK top performance is typically defined as consisting of 'evidence for the capacity for independent thought' and the ability to come up with something that is novel and original. Most supervisors will therefore want to satisfy themselves that you as their student are able to work with a reasonable amount of independence towards the ultimate goal of presenting a piece of work that will make a 'unique, novel' contribution to existing knowledge. If the end goal is to present a piece of work that requires creativity and independence, then supervisors will look for evidence that the student is able to work creatively and independently at the application stage. This means that typically the supervisor will want to have only limited input into the drafting of the proposal or in setting the research questions and direction of the work. Whether you yourself can draft a reasonably coherent proposal is one of the assessment criterions that the supervisor will want to use as evidence to inform their decision whether to take you on. This can pose a problem for students who are used to looking to the teacher for answers. Students from some cultural settings might find the idea that they, the student, should set the direction of the work instead of the teacher quite alien, and they will struggle to do so. However, knowing that this is culturally expected can hopefully help you feel emboldened. Yes, what you propose must tie in with the supervisor's interests, and it must be related to their expertise. At the same time, the proposal should be unmistakably 'yours,' driven by your ideas and interests.

## Cross-cultural differences post-arrival: an East-West example

In my experience, there tends to be a difference in the definition of an 'excellent student' in the minds of many of my Asian (especially Chinese) students and in the minds of Western teachers and the marking schemes at most British (and American) universities. In Britain, what marks students out as top performers according to markers' guidelines and teachers' expectations is not their ability to memorise and correctly reproduce large quantities of factual material, but the top students are set apart by something often described as 'evidence of independent thought.' In the British model, the best students will go beyond the material they have learned and create something new, something novel, something that no one has ever thought of, something that extends the boundaries of knowledge and clearly goes beyond what is written in the textbooks. This 'something new' must be 'original' and unique; it might be a new theory, a new way of resolving apparent contradictions in the literature, a new model, a new solution to a problem that no one has ever thought of before.

These ideas are entirely alien to most Chinese students I have taught over the years. Those often very diligent and ambitious students arrived in the UK from an educational system that had taught them that an excellent student tries to learn off by heart as much of the established facts as possible, and that an excellent student must be deferential to the teacher's superior knowledge. This often leads to considerable confusion in the British classroom, where students – especially at postgraduate level – are encouraged to engage in classroom debate, in defending their views, and in putting forward strong arguments that might deviate not only from each other but also from those advanced by the teacher. I have had many a confused Chinese student in my class who could not understand why I was asking of them to challenge my reasoning: to them, it was clear that I as the teacher have the better grasp of the material and their assumption was that I must therefore be unquestioningly correct in my reading of the facts. Why would I then ask them to contradict me? It can be very hard to explain the Western emphasis on 'independent thought leadership' and 'original contribution' to someone who has been taught to achieve mastery by learning, as well as possible, the ideas proposed by others, and someone who has been taught to be differential to the teacher and to not stick out by voicing individual discordant opinions, which is seen as potentially very rude. Make sure you understand the expectations and the marking criteria. What marks out a performance as 'outstanding' and worthy of a 'distinction'? Are the criteria that you are used to the same that are used in the British cultural context? Make sure you don't work from false assumptions: you can only perform at optimal level if you are fully aware how optimal performance is defined in the British cultural context.

Of course, my description above is a gross generalisation. There are plenty of native British students who also struggle with the meaning of 'original thought,' and there are some Asian students who have adopted very well to the British expectations. Nonetheless, by and large there are clear cultural differences between different parts of the world in how 'excellent performance' is defined. For international students coming to the UK to study, it will be even more important than for home students to consult the marking schemes and seek guidance from their tutors and mentors, to make sure that they understand the expectations and norms.

There are training programmes available in cross-cultural communication that aim to increase intercultural competence and sensitivity to cultural misunderstandings. Such trainings might help participants interact more effectively across diverse cultural contexts. They typically cover self-awareness of cultural biases, differences in verbal and nonverbal communication, and psychological frameworks to understand cultural differences concerning values such as individualism/collectivism, power distance, and time orientation. Trainings usually emphasise active listening, empathy, and strategies for resolving misunderstandings respectfully.

Participants often engage in practical exercises, including role-playing, to practice adapting communication styles, giving feedback, and building rapport. Overall, the training equips individuals with awareness, flexibility, and practical skills to navigate cultural differences, fostering clearer, more respectful, and effective communication in global or multicultural settings. Programmes naturally vary in terms of their quality, but if your chosen university offers this kind of support, it is well worth signing up for.

## Intergroup contact as enriching and instructive

Humans often tend to gravitate to others who are 'like them.' Those who are similar to us are likely to make us feel comfortable because we do not have to work as hard to make ourselves understood. In British classrooms, without fail after the start-of-term induction events different groupings of students form – the British home students tend to stick together, the Chinese students tend to cluster together, and so on. However, just networking with people who are 'like us' limits our horizon. To have a healthy creative and optimally enriching learning process, diversity of views and opinions is often extremely valuable. Students who put effort into networking across cultural boundaries will be rewarded by an expanded horizon and by honed intercultural skills that might well come in handy on the job market post-PhD as well.

Cross-group contact between international and home students also is of broader societal benefit. It is highly valuable for promoting intergroup harmony and reducing stereotypes, as highlighted by Allport's contact hypothesis. According to Allport, meaningful interaction between members of different groups can decrease prejudice, particularly when certain conditions are met: equal status among participants, common goals, cooperation, and institutional support. In a university setting, structured opportunities such as group projects, discussion forums, or social events allow international and home students to engage collaboratively, learn about each other's perspectives, and challenge preconceived notions. Through these interactions, students gain direct experience with cultural diversity, humanising those from different backgrounds and weakening reliance on stereotypes. Additionally, positive contact fosters empathy, mutual respect, and a sense of shared community, which strengthens social cohesion on campus. Overall, facilitating frequent and meaningful cross-group engagement not only enriches students' academic and personal experiences but also contributes to a more inclusive and harmonious university environment, and ultimately society.

Of course, it is difficult for international students to network with natives if those natives are reluctant to reciprocate. This is why teachers and universities should establish clear norms and expectations to encourage inclusion of overseas students in the classroom and extracurricular activities. Subtle exclusion can be experienced as psychologically very damaging and hurtful, and a PhD programme that values EDI will actively work on inclusivity that also encompasses overseas students. Institutions must aspire to establish inclusive and non-discriminatory environments; in fact, they have a legal obligation to do so (at least in the UK), and many have effective policy frameworks to deliver on this. At the end of the day, there are certain things PhD students can do themselves to ensure that their PhD journey is smooth and rewarding, but if contextual factors are not conducive, this will have inevitable negative consequences outside the PhD student's control. What is needed is both the right mindset in the student and the right, supportive environment.

## Top tips

1. Stay alert to the potential of cross-cultural misunderstandings and be ready to troubleshoot when they arise. When difficulties or discomfort arises in interpersonal interactions, don't jump to conclusions but consider how cultural differences might contribute to the situation.
2. British universities place much value on evidence of 'independent thought.' Be mindful of that if you are not used to this from your educational background.
3. More broadly, ensure that you understand the marking criteria and expectations and if necessary, ask for guidance. Criteria might well differ from what you have been used to in the past.
4. Embrace the chance to work with others from diverse cultural contexts: they might be able to offer you perspectives that are entirely new to you. This will be enriching and increase your intercultural awareness and competence.

# 8 Your path to post-PhD success

So now that you are well on your way towards obtaining your PhD, how can you ensure you succeed not only at being awarded the title, but also at securing your dream job afterwards? How do you ensure that you become the most employable graduate you can be, with the strongest profile of transferable skills and achievements that count on the job market?

## The importance of clearly defined career goals

One major decision you will have to make is if you want to stay in academia or leave to work in industry, the third sector, or if you have yet other goals. Moreover, even if you have decided that you want to stay in academia, there are yet more decisions to make: there are many different types of contracts, and you will need to decide which tract is most appealing to you. This is an important choice because it informs what profile you should build throughout your PhD journey and beyond.

It might be helpful to provide a brief overview of job types within academia. The 'classic' academic role is one that includes both Teaching and Research, as well as an expectation to contribute to some internal admin/leadership and the university's self-governance, for example by taking responsibility for strategic briefs like the coordination of exam boards, student recruitment, outreach, curriculum development, and the like. Before landing such a tenure-track position, many applicants need to spend some time working as a PostDoc. These are usually time-limited, research-only appointments, most commonly working on delivering an externally funded research grant awarded to an academic. In addition, most universities in the UK offer teaching-only contracts. These can be temporary or permanent positions that do not have an expectation of bringing in external research funding attached to them. Universities differ in the way they are set up: some teaching-focused posts might have a well-mapped out career trajectory up to Professor, while some posts do not have clear career progression opportunities built in. In addition to these

DOI: 10.4324/9781003630074-8

different contract types, there are also in some institutions other arrangements such as professional practice contracts (whereby an employee is expected to have their academic work informed by their applied professional practice, for example work as a clinical psychologist). In especially lab-heavy disciplines, a PhD can also lead to an appointment as a technical operations manager, someone who makes sure the labs are run safely and efficiently and optimally used for research and teaching. Finally, some PhD graduates find employment at universities on the 'professional services' side rather than the academic side, working in student administration, student support, alumni relations, and fundraising, for example. What I am describing is not a comprehensive list of all employment types and opportunities, and it is focused on the UK system – other countries will offer variations on what is summarised here.

The vacancies open to PhD graduates in industry will obviously depend on the discipline. Options are wide-ranging and might include virtually any field or industry. To give a flavour, if I think of positions some of our recent social psychology PhD students have taken up outside academia, these include the civil service (fast-track leadership route), freelancing as an organisational change and development consultant, working for a marketing and image consultancy agency, user experience roles in social media companies, market research, and monitoring and evaluation specialist roles in the international development sector. What is clear is that a PhD can open an entire range of different doors, which can make the next step both exciting and a little daunting.

If you want to leave academia after your PhD, then you might be best advised to spend your energy not on getting your work published in the highest impact factor journals, but on gaining work experience during an industry placement – the general benefits of doing this was already covered briefly in Chapter 1. If you want to stay in academia, there are still more decisions to make: do you aspire to go into a teaching-focused career, or do you want to be research active? Are you happy with the prospect of doing one or several short (2–3 year) PostDoc positions to boost your publication profile, even if those positions mean moving between cities and maybe even countries? For someone who is serious about building a stellar publication record, the PostDoc route can be an attractive option, but you might have domestic, caring, or other responsibilities that mean that the level of geographic mobility this choice entails is not a realistic option for you. Whatever choice you make, it is important that you talk to your PhD supervisor about your end goal, because the destination goal has implications for how you make best use of your time during your PhD.

Of course, sometimes goals change. Students often end up graduating with quite different ideas about their future than they had when they originally enrolled. This is fine – a PhD degree is an opportunity to learn, grown, and try things, after all. The point I'm making is not that you need to define your goal and stick to it no matter what. The point is rather that it will pay off to periodically reflect on your longer-term goals, evaluate whether they need updating, and work out the implications of your end goals for your day-to-day management of your time.

Do you feel that it is kind of obvious that you should be thinking about your end goal, and that this goal should inform the steps you take towards this goal? I agree, it should be obvious! However, it seems even though this is self-evident, sadly it is easy to lose perspective in the day-to-day muddle and demands that come with doing any job. Anyone who has ever taken part in an endless meeting that seems pointless, and anyone who has ever had to complete an endless bureaucratic form where the sole purpose seemed to be to waste time, will know: we often end up doing stuff that seems pointless and a waste of time, because not enough people regularly ask themselves the question: why are we doing this? Is it goal-directed, and are the opportunity costs (the things you forsake that you could achieve if you chose a different approach) justified? Is this the best way to achieve what we want to achieve? Are we on track? Let's work to make sure that your activity is goal-directed and that the way you spend your energy day-to-day is aligned with your long-term goals.

## SMART PhD objectives tie your day-to-day activities to your end goal

One approach that is often used in project management is the setting of so-called 'SMART objectives,' and this is also useful when thinking about goal setting during your PhD. Smart objectives are 'specific, measurable, achievable, (sometimes the 'A' is interpreted to stand for 'agreed' instead), realistic (or relevant) and time-bound (or timely).' Goals need to be specific because vague things tend to not happen. An objective of 'I must make sure I work more on my PhD' is much less likely to achieve the desired outcome than an objective of 'every weekday from 10 until 3 I will work on my PhD except Fridays, which I will take off.' An objective must be measurable, so that it is possible to monitor progress towards it. In many ways, measurability comes with specificity: as soon as you make goals concrete and specific, it is much easier to monitor whether you are achieving the objectives or not.

An especially important feature of a sensible and useful PhD goal is that it must be achievable. We have already talked about the fact that PhD students often have an eye on what has not yet been achieved rather than what has been achieved, and the fact that it is always possible to publish more and in better journals, and to be more recognised for one's work, to receive more prizes and invitations to give keynotes, etc. Because there is no natural upper limit to what can theoretically be achieved, there is a risk that endless striving becomes too extreme and exhausting. A further factor that might entice PhD students to set unrealistically ambitious goals are the cultural norms within higher education which socialise academics into a mindset whereby professional and personal fulfilment are conflated. For many academics, their work is also their passion, the thing that gives meaning and fulfilment to their lives – and meaning and pleasure are the two essential components of human happiness. There are few other occupations where the conflation between the personal and the professional is so extreme, and these norms invite many academics to work exceptionally long hours and to work at the weekends. If your work is your passion, why wouldn't you want to pursue it on Saturdays? Boundaries become blurred. Of course, if work is not only a means to earning a living but also something that gives happiness, then work becomes imbued with incredible importance. And things that are important get a lot of energy spent on them – we want to make sure that important goals are optimised, ambitious, emphasised, competitive. The importance of PhD students' work goals in relation to both work and personal functions means that students might be tempted to strive for the unattainable – if it matters that much, it must be perfect. Because of these potential pitfalls, it is especially important that PhD goals that are set are achievable and not unrealistic and overly ambitious. Failure to calibrate correctly what is achievable can lead to burn-out, as discussed in Chapter 5.

Having said all this, the 'A' in SMART is sometimes taken to stand not for 'achievable' but for 'agreed,' which is of almost equal importance. Your life as a PhD student will be made easier if you and your supervisor or supervisory team are on the same page with regard to what needs to be achieved and by when. Many a supervisory arrangement has broken down because of a mismatch of assumptions regarding the objectives. If your supervisor does not by themselves volunteer to agree goals for your PhD, you should prompt them. Ask them what is expected of you and agree a mutual plan that challenges you but that is realistic, and that you have both signed up to. An actionable plan includes both the end goal and stage goals – you need clarity of what your supervisor wants you to deliver next week, next month, next year. If this is not clear to you, ask for clarification.

Let's now turn to the 'R' in Smart. We saw above that 'specific' and 'measurable' features of goals are related to each other, and in the same way 'achievable' and 'realistic' goals are related. Goals are realistic if they carefully consider the time and resources at hand, and if practical constraints are used as guidance for what can be expected in terms of outputs. Considering realistic boundary conditions with open eyes will ensure that goals remain achievable. One of the most common bits of feedback I give to students, especially at the start of their PhD journeys, is that their plans are not realistic. Students often have a much keener eye for the 'ideal' of what they want to do than for the 'practical.' They suggest collecting data from large samples, hard-to-reach populations, and to test ideas that are wide-ranging enough to make for a life's work rather than just a PhD. When I ask them how they plan to collect the data, how they will access the participants, or how they will realise their lofty ambitions within a short three-year period, they are dumbfounded. To complete your PhD successfully, a healthy dose of pragmatism is needed alongside some idealism needed to carry you through.

Having said this, the 'R' in SMART is sometimes taken to stand for 'relevant,' which makes it my favourite feature of smart objective setting. It is my observation that often the day-to-day activity of students is not well connected to their end goals, and when there is a disconnect between micro activity and macro goal then a situation arises where energy is spent on the wrong things, on things that should not be prioritised or that don't actually matter. Being clear about your end goal – and keeping this goal in mind and reviewing it regularly – is essential to ensuring that the micro-goals that function as stepping stones towards the larger goal remain relevant.

Last but not least, SMART PhD goals are time-bound (or timely). This means that you don't only define what needs doing, but also the timeframe in which you aim to achieve certain objectives. This is a vital exercise to ensure that you keep on track and that your goals remain overall realistic and achievable. If your PhD supervisor does not suggest it, then make sure that you define the time-boundness of your activities yourself: make yourself a Gantt chart or draft timetable of what you want to achieve by when and monitor your progress against that plan.

## Be clear on the knowledge, skills, abilities, and attributes you need for your dream job

Desirable attributions for applicants to vacancies differ considerably between academic and industry jobs. Do take the time to peruse some job descriptions and person specifications for positions you might be interested in in the future, and think about how you meet those criteria or how you can strengthen your profile to ensure that you meet them upon completion of your PhD.

For example, if you were to aim for an academic role, then the most important aspect to work on, by a mile, is your publication record. Just having a PhD degree is usually not enough, given today's highly competitive market: for entry positions in academia, junior scholars nowadays need to have an impressive publication track record. If this is what you are aiming for, then you should ask your supervisor for advice and support on how to maximise your chances of obtaining publications. They might be able to involve you in ongoing projects they are leading, for example, and give you credit for your input in the form of co-authorship on a paper. To obtain academic positions, it can also be helpful to network and to organise research lab visits with leaders in the field. If the goal is an academic position, then it will also be useful to gain experience in some of the key tasks and duties academics carry out, for example getting experience in how to peer review papers or acquiring data analytical skills that are relevant specifically to your field. These are activities that are probably not so valuable for PhD candidates who plan to leave the ivory tower, and if you are aiming for a job in industry, you would be better advised focusing your efforts elsewhere (e.g., placements and work experience). So, this is a good example of where a clearly defined end goal can inform what you might choose to do with your time on a day-to-day basis during your PhD.

If you are clear in your mind that you want to leave academia eventually, it will also pay off to consider where you are headed and how you can best strengthen your profile en route. For example, many PhD students get a choice in whether they want to tutor undergraduate students or not. If you are thinking about going into teaching, this will be something you will definitely want to get involved with, whereas if your dream is to become a financial analyst, this experience will be much less relevant.

Another relevant consideration is that PhD students are often, in theory, able to go for positions that are more senior than graduate-level entry positions by virtue of their additional training. However, there can be some skills and prior experience that are required at higher levels of seniority that PhD students might not have had the chance to get practice in. I recently had a PhD student who was interested in joining a company at a senior level and they met all the criteria in the person spec, except the criterion of prior experience in team management. As mentioned in Chapter 5, doing a PhD is often solitary, and even if PhD students work in a team with peers, they often end up being unable to point to experience in managing a team that reports to them. So, if you think your chosen career will require team management experience, for example, then you would be well advised to ask your supervisor how you can acquire that during your PhD training. Maybe your supervisor is involved in working with groups of students, and this responsibility can be delegated to you? Maybe there is a conference to organise with the help of a team of student assistants, and you can ask to be put in charge of this?

Whatever the criteria, it pays to be clear on the skills and experiences you do want to acquire and to think about what you can do towards achieving this. As suggested above, looking at some job adverts of positions you might be interested in post-PhD is a good starting point. Even better, if you know someone who has recently successfully landed a type of job you might be interested in, do ask them for their CV and application. Many universities also have extensive alumni networks and provide opportunities for students to connect with previous trailblazers during live events or on social media. These are invaluable networking opportunities to make the best out of. Talking to others who have successfully done what you hope to do will not only give you an idea of the profile you need to build, but this can also be an important reality check: given what you expect to have achieved at the end of your PhD, is walking straight into a permanent academic post a realistic goal? Is entering industry at mid-management level a realistic goal? If you are not clear on what you can do to achieve your goals, do ask peers in your network and also your supervisor for guidance: they might just be able to offer valuable advice.

In sum, think about it as a four-step process, as illustrated in Figure 8.1. The first step is to work out what it is you want to do. This is the step where you might benefit from guidance and support. Career advisors at university can administer tests to establish your profile of personal strengths and preferences and then advise you, for example, to step into a 'people facing' role, a role where systematic working is required, or a role where creativity is essential. Working out your ultimate career goal is not an easy feat, especially because the profile of PhD candidates can be very varied: some people are drawn to further study because they like to read and think analytically, some people are drawn to further study because they like the prospect of thought leadership and maybe even fame, some people are drawn to further study because they like the creativity that comes with the process of scientific discovery, some people are drawn to further study

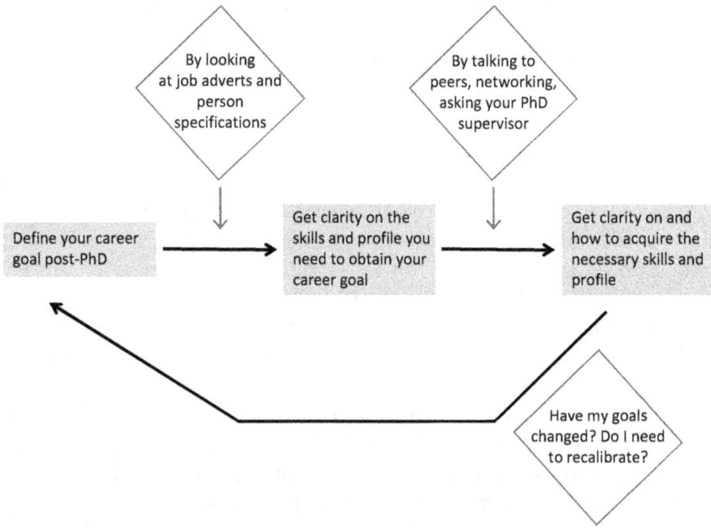


*Figure 8.1* Working towards your Post-PhD career goals.

because they like being their own boss. In short, many types of people embark on doing a PhD, and you will need to work out what floats your boat the most.

Once you have worked out your career goal, the second step is to work out what skills and profile you need to be competitive on the job market. Reading job descriptions and person specifications can give you a clearer idea, as will reading the CV and application documents of peers who have successfully landed a job similar to the one that you aspire to.

Once you know what profile you need, the third step is to work out how to acquire that profile. Asking for advice from people in your network who are knowledgeable in that field is always a good idea. Useful suggestions can also come from your supervisor. If it is more or better publications that you need to work on, they will have suggestions for sure. If it is experience in team working or coding skills or other skills that can be addressed in CPD initiatives such as media training, they might also have useful suggestions on what to sign up for to further strengthen your profile.

The fourth and last step of the process is to re-calibrate regularly (e.g., every six months, you can set yourself a calendar reminder) whether your goals are still current. In this step, you ask yourself: am I still aiming for that career, or have my preferences changed, and is there actually something else that takes my fancy now? Moreover, am I on track to reach my chosen goal, or does this objective not seem realistic given where I am right now, and would I be better off aiming for something else? What I have made a pledge for in this chapter is the importance of bearing your end goal in mind. However, it is still true that your PhD is an opportunity for exploration and playing around with different options and goals, so do keep an open mind. Many students goals change as they go through the PhD process, and that is just fine. Many people now have multiple careers too, where our working life is long enough to satisfy more than one professional curiosity. What will you do after your PhD? Whatever it is, good luck, the world is your oyster.

## Bridging the gap from academia to industry

The transition from doctoral study to industry has increasingly become a key focus for researchers, universities, employers, and policymakers. Only around 30% of PhD students ultimately remain in academia, emphasising why it is crucial for doctoral candidates to consider how their training can be translated into broader employment markets. Historically, British universities – particularly elite institutions like Oxford, Cambridge, and the Russell Group – have celebrated research for its intellectual and cultural value, emphasising curiosity-driven inquiry. This aligns with the classical model of the university as a place for knowledge creation without immediate utilitarian purpose, an ideal that is still more strongly upheld in some other European countries. For example, an ideal central to higher education in Germany is the Humboldt ideal which poses the primary purpose of a university as the pursuit of knowledge for its own sake, emphasising academic freedom, research-led teaching, and the cultivation of intellectual and moral development over vocational or economic outcomes. According to this view, the primary purpose of academic work is to satisfy intellectual curiosity and theoretical advancement, and value is placed on the intrinsic merit of deep inquiry. The creation of new knowledge, even if abstract or seemingly removed from practical application, is considered a central societal contribution in itself.

However, over the past few decades in the UK, the cultural and policy zeitgeist has shifted, with a stronger emphasis on outcome-driven research. Government policies, funding frameworks (e.g., UK Research and Innovation's impact-focused funding), and initiatives like the Research Excellence Framework (REF) increasingly reward work that demonstrates measurable societal or economic impact. The UK government's Skills Agenda and related strategies reinforce this trend, expecting higher education to contribute directly to innovation, productivity, and social benefit. Increasingly, the expectation is that PhD research should demonstrate a tangible positive impact on society or the economy and lead to measurable outcomes, such as innovations, policy influence, technological advancements, or contributions to regional and national growth. This transition reflects a broader societal demand for accountability and utility in higher education and aligning scholarly work with societal needs. Consequently, doctoral training now often incorporates pathways to translate knowledge into real-world applications, bridging academia and industry.

This shift, together with the fact that there are simply fewer job opportunities in British academia today than at other points in the past, means that only a small proportion of PhD students now stay within academia to take up academic roles, and the majority of researchers now take their skills into industry, public policy, entrepreneurship, and other non-academic sectors.

The analytical rigour, problem-solving abilities, quick learning and adaptability, technical expertise, ability to challenge assumptions, communication and project management skills, creativity, and research expertise gained during PhD study are precisely the kinds of skills, capabilities, and experiences many industry organisations need. There are many other transferable skills (some industry specific, some generic) you might acquire during your PhD that are relevant to your chosen industry, and it is well worth researching into this. Often, students need support in order to identify and articulate their competencies into language that resonates with non-academic employers. Industry often focuses on deliverables, commercial outcomes, stakeholder engagement, and cross-functional teamwork, language and priorities many PhD students have little exposure to in academia. Some PhD funding avenues now incorporate industry placements as an integral part of the training route, to empower students in gaining practical industry exposure and experience through internships, thereby easing the transition. Some universities also have careers services and academic initiatives that offer events to support the development of transferable skills through workshops, mentorship schemes, and participation in structured initiatives such as Knowledge Transfer Partnerships (KTPs) and Doctoral Training Partnerships (DTPs) – programmes that embed researchers within companies to tackle real innovation challenges and build industry experience. Such opportunities can be incredibly useful and enhance your future career prospects – do make use of them where you can. Engaging with them can enhance your translational thinking and demonstrate proactive career planning.

There are a few practical steps you can take already during your PhD to prepare you for future industry interviews. Defining your career goals outside academia early on will help identify and audit your relevant skills, to close any knowledge gaps, and to start building a strategic network. Do you have any friends who went into that industry post-PhD? Does the university have any alumni networks that might provide you with helpful links? Conversations with others who are one or two steps ahead of you in your chosen career path can be very valuable. They can also help you hone your 'story' – contacts can give you very useful feedback on what your strengths are, how to communicate them, and where to enhance them if needed.

## International students: unique considerations

International students wishing to remain in the UK after completing their studies have several pathways to post-study career success, with the Graduate Visa scheme being a primary mechanism (at the time of writing). This visa allows graduates to work, or seek work, for two to three years depending on the level of qualification, offering a valuable period to gain professional experience. Career opportunities span academia, research, industry, and professional services, where employers often value the global perspective, adaptability, and cross-cultural skills that international graduates bring. Strategic approaches to securing employment include actively networking with alumni, attending university career fairs, participating in internships or work placements during study, and leveraging university career services. Tailoring applications to meet UK workplace expectations – particularly in communication, teamwork, and evidence of initiative – is critical.

However, international graduates face notable challenges. Visa restrictions may limit long-term employment options without employer sponsorship, and competition with domestic graduates can be intense. Many students seek to use the Graduate Visa scheme as a launching pad from which to try to secure employer sponsorship to enable more long-term UK employment, but chances of success are not guaranteed. Moreover, cultural and workplace norms may differ significantly from those in the student's home country, affecting communication styles, hierarchy, and professional expectations. Proactively seeking mentorship, understanding industry-specific requirements, and demonstrating both technical competence and cultural adaptability are essential strategies to overcome these challenges. Familiarity with UK professional networks, including professional bodies and sector-specific associations, can also enhance employability and career progression.

For international students planning to return to their home country, a UK degree can be a strong differentiator in the job market. International experience often signals advanced skills, independence, and exposure to global best practices, which can be advantageous in leadership, research, and specialised professional roles. Students can capitalise on these benefits by maintaining connections with UK-based professors, peers, and professional contacts, which may facilitate collaborative projects or access to international networks.

Challenges in returning home often revolve around readjusting to local workplace cultures and demonstrating the relevance of UK-acquired skills. This is particularly the case for work in more highly regulated industries such as engineering, medicine, or mental health. I could write a whole chapter or maybe even book on the conditions under which different types of UK psychology degrees (UG, PGT/MSc, PGR/PhD, DClinPsy) may or may not allow the graduate to work in different mental health settings and roles in the UK as well as various other countries globally! The key message to students is that the transnational transferability of accredited degree credentials can be complex and should be carefully researched before international study is embarked on, to ensure education aligns with eventual career goals.

Reverse culture shock may affect both personal and professional adaptation, while local employers may have limited understanding of UK educational or research practices. To navigate these challenges, graduates should translate their skills and experiences into locally recognised competencies, seek guidance from returning alumni, and actively engage with professional networks in their home country. By strategically bridging international experience and local expectations, graduates can maximise the impact of their UK education while easing reintegration into domestic work environments.

Last but not least, life is not only about work and optimising one's academic and career outcomes. Whilst quietly working towards a degree, life continues to happen. Many PhD students embark on their studies during a time where they are of an age where people fall in love accidentally or where they are looking to find stable partners and start a family. If you are abroad whilst settling down, chances are you might spend a significant part of your life in that country. I have seen this happen to many international PhD students. I also know one person who relocated back to the UK from Australia, precisely in order to avoid settling down in Australia in the long run during a period in her life where 'settling down' was clearly a priority! Few people have this discipline and foresight. Whatever your life plans, try to make your career choices with open eyes for the intended as well as potentially unintended consequences.

## Top tips

1. Decide early on if you want to stay in academia or go to industry, and what kind of position you are interested in. Keep an open mind and review your choice but give it some thought right from the start.
2. Make sure your PhD objectives are SMART and tied to your career end goal. Your ultimate career goals should define how you spend your time day-to-day during your PhD.
3. If you are not clear about the skills and experiences that are needed for your career goal, or how to obtain them, do your research: look at job adverts, ask your peers, and ask your supervisors.
4. Once you know about the profile that is required, seek clarity on how you can acquire the necessary skills and attributes. If the path to that goal is not obvious to you, ask your supervisor and mentors for input.
5. Every six months or so, walk through the four-step process outlined in Figure 8.1: (1) reflect on your end goal in terms of career choice post-PhD; (2) determine the skills, experience, and profile you need to acquire to be competitive for this type of position; (3) work out how you can acquire the necessary skills; and (4) regularly assess if your goals are still up-to-date or if your preferences have changed.

# 9 Parting words

To sum up, this book focuses on the human, psychological, and relational dimensions of undertaking a PhD, rather than on disciplinary research methods or technical aspects of doctoral work. Central to the book is an exploration of emotions, identity, motivation, confidence-building, and resilience required during doctoral study. It does not provide instruction on conducting literature reviews, data analysis, or specific research methodologies – there are other reference works available which focus more on the 'nuts and bolts' of the work. Instead, this book addresses the often underexplored experiences that shape doctoral success and well-being. Foregrounding the psychology of doing a PhD is not accidental – after all, the author is a psychologist! And a psychologist specialising on discrimination, interethnic relations, and structural barriers based on group membership, for that matter. The focus on inclusivity and broadening access for those who have traditionally been excluded from higher study is therefore no accident. This book, then, intends to support current and prospective PhD students by drawing on my decade-long experience in student supervision and highlighting both pathways to greater inclusivity and the importance of human processes and relationships on the road to PhD success. By demystifying the doctoral journey, the book aims to support students to achieve a more inclusive and humane doctoral experience.

The advice is based on my experience of working with a diverse cohort of doctoral students. However, invaluable insights can also be gleamed from what successful students themselves say about their experience. To this end, I asked some of my recent graduates three questions: What was the biggest challenge you faced during your PhD? What advice would you give someone considering a PhD? And what did you like best about doing a PhD? Here's a brief summary of what my students said.

## Advice from my former PhD students

In terms of challenges that had to be overcome, this was some of the feedback:

DOI: 10.4324/9781003630074-9

> The most challenging thing for me was that sometimes I feel too overwhelmed. It's a good thing to have the freedom you don't have during your undergrad. Everything is clearer during your undergrad; the instructions are mostly precise… During PhD, you will realize that many things are controversial in academia. I think it is sometimes not clear what to do.

Another student said:

> The isolation, and the high expectations (that often you can create for yourself too). And sometimes the fast-paced nature of a 3-year PhD means you might feel rushed into doing something early on which you look back to once you have developed further as a researcher and have more experience, you think of many other ways you could have done it differently. Although that offers a great learning opportunity, it can be challenging at times to navigate.

Another student said:

> One of the most difficult things has been developing structure. Doing a PhD has many advantages, one of which is the amount of flexibility to my working hours. But there are also a lot of other responsibilities and expectations that come with doing a PhD. For example, training, attending talks/conferences, teaching responsibilities, etc… All of these things together can often feel incredibly overwhelming and make it hard to have a structured working pattern. It can also feel very isolating because as a PhD student there's no exact comparison or point of reference with other students. For instance, when doing an undergraduate degree everyone else is doing the same course as you – so you can often gauge how you are doing compared to others, you can see whether there are others struggling with the same aspects of the course as you. It's not possible to do this with a PhD because every PhD is different and everyone is working to a different timeline, etc.

There are some clear themes that emerge from the above. The first one is around challenges posed by lack of structure. This can be in relation to ideas – advanced study brings the realisation that things are nuanced and not black and white, and that it is often unclear what the right way to think about things or approach things is. It can also be about routine – PhD work offers great freedom about how one's work should be scheduled and what routine works best for you, but this lack of structure also causes uncertainty because students have to build the 'scaffolding' of their work themselves. This is why, in Chapter 3, I talked about the importance of establishing a healthy work-life balance and routine, and defending it.

The second theme is around isolation and loneliness. Indeed, your PhD journey is your own, and no one else is on exactly the same journey. This can be exciting but also lonely. This is why, in Chapter 5, I talked about different ways in which loneliness can be combated and the importance of teamwork and investing in strong social networks. It is also why, in Chapter 4, I talked about ways in which to ensure a strong and healthy working relationship with your supervisor. Your supervisor is on your journey with you, they are probably the one person in your life who have the best understanding of the sights you are seeing en route and the bumps in the road you are encountering. As such, if they are good at their job, they might be able to offer some emotional as well as subject-specific support along the way.

The third theme that emerges is that students were keen to emphasise that challenges are opportunities for growth. Indeed, this is what a PhD journey – or any educational journey for that matter – is about: navigating new ideas, new problems, new contexts, which leads to intellectual, personal, and professional growth. Growth is inseparable from challenge because development requires disruption of existing habits, assumptions, and capacities. Without encountering difficulty, uncertainty, or resistance, there is no impetus to adapt, reflect, or acquire new ways of thinking and acting. And PhD study offers plenty of opportunity for challenge-induced growth.

In terms of advice my students had for prospective students, this is what they said:

> The most important thing that I can recommend is to build sustainable habits and routines. For example, discovering when or where you are more productive. It's important to work effectively rather than extensively. I also believe taking care of your body is very important. Sometimes people can devote all their time to work, but I think this is not wise. Excise and a healthy diet help you to focus and work better. You become more efficient. Lastly, it is crucial to have a keen interest in your topic. It is vital because you will work on that topic most of your time. Also, you need to contribute to that field, meaning that you need to be creative and find the gaps in the field. If you are not really that interested, this will be harder.

Another piece of advice was:

> My advice would be to make sure that they are genuinely interested in the area and the process of undertaking research and critical thinking. I would also advise organisation and writing from early on to help you in the future.

Another student's take was this:

> The most important thing I would advise is developing a structure that works for you. The flexibility of doing a PhD means that it can often be tempting to put things off or on the backburner for weeks on end. Having a structure to your days helps keep on top of things. This structure must be self-tailored because what works for other PhD students might not work for you. It helps to know whether you work best with lots of mini breaks through the day or just one long break. Whether you're more productive working 5 days a week 9–5 or you prefer less conventional working hours. I have personally found it incredibly useful to map out my working day by writing out everything I needed to get done that day. You then select the three most important things – those that are a priority to get done and dedicate time to do these. This has really helped me structure my working days and it also meant that at the very least, I got 3 important tasks done each day.

Unsurprisingly, the key pieces of advice that my students flagged relate to some of the key challenges they identified. A key theme that emerged once again was related to structure and routine, both in terms of the writing process, i.e., the work itself, and the working routine. Students felt it was really important to impose a structure to help with navigating the journey. All three quotes above emphasised this, which illustrates just how central this challenge is perceived to be by many PhD students.

A further common theme is the importance of genuine interest in the research topic. This is a key point I always make to prospective students; it is something they must ponder before they embark on the journey. Ask yourself: do I care so deeply about this issue that I want to devote three years of my life to it? The focused nature of PhD work, together with the long timeframe needed to reach the end goal, requires a high level of dedication, higher than for most other professional pursuits. The closest analogy I can think of is the dedication required from professional musicians or athletes – they, too, must put in long hours over a very extended period of time, in a single-minded way and to the exclusion of other interests/pursuits, in order to reach their goals. This requires discipline, dedication, grit, perseverance, and resilience. This combination of traits is rare. However, these are also attributes that can be acquired – after a successful PhD, many students will be more resilient than before, and they will have developed grit that they can usefully apply to future challenges. Moreover, the central thesis of this book is that most people who desire to do so can succeed at PhD study, given that the right contextual scaffolding is in place. For example, I have seen many students who did not naturally have the self-discipline to impose structure on their work and who required the support of their supervisors to help them with this. Those students, as they moved through their PhD, learned to get better at self-imposed discipline. A PhD is a learning process, and one that you will succeed at if you are lucky or smart enough to ensure that you benefit from a supportive environment and if you have open eyes for the potential pitfalls and are equipped with tools to address them. Hopefully this book can help with this in a small way.

Finally, when asked about what they liked best about doing a PhD, this is what my students had to say: 'The thing I liked the most about doing PhD is I like that I could test my own ideas. The best part is you have supervisors who guide you while allowing that. It's great because you learn many things.' Another student added:

> The best thing about doing a PhD is having the freedom to explore research questions and experience undertaking research from the very beginning to the end - presenting output and also trying to engage with wider stakeholders to try and actually make an impact with your findings.

A final take on the question was this:

> The thing I liked best about doing a PhD is that I got to investigate topics that I care about and/or find intriguing. There's something incredibly satisfying about being able to devise experiments to find answers to questions. In addition to satiating my curiosities, there's also a hope that my research will have some kind of impact – be it through prejudice reduction interventions, informing policy, or just adding more insight on these issues. Being a PhD student gives you the opportunity to work on something that is important to you. As such, even though it is hard work – there's an added sense of purpose which (for me at least) helps fuel motivation and willingness to do the work.

There are some beautiful themes coming through in these quotes which will resonate with many PhD students – these are centred around creativity, freedom, learning, and impact. PhD-level study is about scientific discovery and making a unique contribution. At its core, a doctorate invites creativity not as an optional extra, but as a necessity: researchers must generate original ideas, design novel approaches, and find innovative solutions to complex problems that often have no clear answers. This creative process is closely tied to the freedom inherent in PhD study. Unlike more structured educational pathways, doctoral research allows scholars significant autonomy to shape their questions, methods, and intellectual direction, encouraging independent thinking and ownership over one's work. This freedom fosters a strong sense of intrinsic motivation, as progress is driven not by rigid curricula but by curiosity and personal investment in the research topic. As mentioned elsewhere in the book, the exact nature of PhD-level study varies between countries. For example, in the USA the emphasis on class-based instruction is higher and the emphasis on discovery-driven individual research is lower than in the UK. Supervisors also differ in terms of how much room they give their students to explore creatively versus how many clear intellectual guardrails they provide for their work. Nonetheless, it is a universal truth that PhD-level work offers higher degrees of freedom and creativity than any other level of study.

Alongside creativity and freedom, continuous learning is one of the most rewarding aspects of PhD study. Doctoral candidates engage in deep, sustained learning that extends beyond acquiring knowledge to mastering critical thinking, problem-solving, and intellectual resilience. The process involves grappling with uncertainty, refining arguments, and integrating feedback, all of which contribute to profound intellectual growth. Importantly, this learning is cumulative and transformative, reshaping how scholars understand their field and how they approach questions more broadly.

Perhaps most fulfilling is the potential for impact that PhD study offers. By contributing original research, doctoral scholars expand the boundaries of human knowledge, whether through advancing theory, improving practical applications, influencing policy, or addressing societal challenges. Even when the impact is incremental, the knowledge that one's work may inform future research, benefit communities, or shape understanding provides a strong sense of purpose for many PhD students. The combination of creative exploration, intellectual freedom, deep learning, and meaningful impact makes PhD-level study not merely an academic qualification, but a profoundly enriching experience that aligns personal curiosity with making a lasting – if small – contribution to society.

## Final words

A PhD is for everyone. Everyone who likes to think deeply about things, everyone who is ambitious and likes a challenge, and everyone who is interested in advanced postgraduate education to enhance their profile on the job market inside and outside academia. If this sounds like you, then a PhD is for you. No one should be held back from achieving a PhD because of their background. A world where some people are taught to aspire to more and to aim higher than others is deeply unfair. A world where some people are given a key to academic opportunities whilst others have the door shut in their face is flawed. Everyone who wants to do a PhD should be able to have access to this opportunity, no matter who they are. This book aims to make a small contribution towards this goal – it is a psychologist's guide on how to navigate the PhD journey. The book aims to broaden accessibility of higher education for those who are not already 'in the know.' The book also aims to give courage to students from historically disadvantaged backgrounds and those coming from different cultures. Academia is no longer a place for old white men; it is a place for you, no matter who you are. I wish you the best of luck on your PhD journey.

# Index

Pages in **bold** refer to tables

www.ingramcontent.com/pod-product-compliance
Lightning Source LLC
LaVergne TN
LVHW011029110826
845149LV00015B/3340